FOR~PROFIT HIGHER EDUCATION

FOR-PROFIT HIGHER EDUCATION

DEVELOPING A WORLD-CLASS WORKFORCE

JOHN SPERLING &
ROBERT W. TUCKER

Transaction Publishers
New Brunswick (U.S.A.) and London (U.K.)

This book is printed on acid-free paper that meets the American National Standard for Permanence of Paper for Printed Library Materials.

Library of Congress Catalog Number: 96-41181
ISBN: 1-56000-306-5 (cloth); 1-56000-937-3 (paper)
Printed in the United States of America

Library of Congress Cataloging-in-Publication Data

Sperling, John G.
For-profit higher education : developing a world-class workforce / John Sperling, Robert W. Tucker.
p. cm.
Includes bibliographical references and index.
ISBN 1-56000-306-5 (cloth : alk. paper). — 1-56000-937-3 (pbk. : alk. paper)
1. Continuing education—United States. 2. Adult education—United States. 3. Professional education—United States. 4. Proprietary schools—United States. 5. Education, Higher-Economic aspects—United States. 6. University of Phoenix. I. Tucker, Robert W. II. Title.
LC5251.S66 1996
374'.973—dc20 96-41181
[374'.013] CIP

Contents

Preface

The authors of this book hold, or have held, positions with the University of Phoenix (UOP) and its sister company, the Institute for Professional Development (IPD). IPD assists regionally accredited colleges and universities in establishing programs for working adults that are based on a unique teaching/learning model for working adults in higher education. The structure and operations of these two organizations and how they differ from other traditional and nontraditional institutions has been the focus of our research, and this research is the source of most of our policy recommendations.

The current operations of the University of Phoenix reflect what we call the UOP Model and it is this model that we contrast with the structure and operations of other programs, whether they are traditional or nontraditional. This focus is pragmatic and not ideological. There are few institutions that have the same mission—the education of working adults—in business, management, computer science, nursing, counseling, education, and a variety of specializations within these professions—as does UOP. There are none that are for-profit. To the best of our knowledge, UOP is the only adult-centered institution with all of the characteristics we believe are essential in meeting the educational needs of those working adults who aspire to professional positions.

The readers of our various drafts have assured us that the positions we set forth in this book are controversial and sure to be challenged by members of the larger academic community. Lest we be accused of being self-serving in the arguments we present, we believe it wise to inform the reader of our biases. Many of our academic friends and former colleagues from traditional institutions generously gave this book a critical reading and we are indebted to them for a host of well-founded changes. However, one change, which most of them recommended, we have chosen not to adopt. This was the recommendation to excise the argument in favor of a for-profit institutional structure as the preferred structure for the adult-centered university. Our academic critics have pointed out that favoring a for-profit corporate structure would appear self-serving since the for-profit University of Phoenix is our exemplar. This is a serious criticism that must be addressed up front.

The prototype of the UOP Model was introduced in 1973 at the University of San Francisco by IPD, which three years later established the University of Phoenix. In the ensuing twenty-three years, the model has been under constant change and, we hope, improvement. However, through all of the changes, certain fundamental elements have remained unchanged:

- working professionals and those who aspire to professional positions are the target population;
- all of the faculty are working professionals who are trained in the skills needed to deliver the curriculum;
- the curriculum is centrally produced by faculty members working with professional course designers and curriculum editors;
- the curriculum is outcome driven;
- both cognitive and affective learning outcomes are assessed;
- classes are small, averaging 15 students, and all students belong to study groups of three to five members;
- all aspects of the model are guided toward gradual improvement by a quality management system;
- the students are viewed as valued customers and treated accordingly; and
- the enterprise is governed as an academic institution and managed as a for-profit business.

During these twenty-three years, some form of the UOP Model was adopted by the following colleges and universities, which contracted with IPD to create for them a system of education for working adults. Institutions are listed in the order in which the IPD contracts became effective:

1. University of San Francisco, CA
2. Saint Mary's College, Moraga, CA
3. University of Redlands, Redlands, CA
4. Elmhurst College, Elmhurst, IL
5. National Louis University, Evanston, IL
6. Regis University, Denver, CO
7. Lesley College, Boston, MA
8. Tusculum College, Tusculum, TN
9. Cardinal Stritch College, Milwaukee, WI

10. Indiana Wesleyan University, Marion, IN
11. Central Wesleyan College, Central, SC
12. Averett College, Danville, VA
13. Baker University, Baldwin City, KS
14. LeTourneau University, Longview, TX
15. Eastern Nazarene College, Boston, MA
16. Olivet Nazarene University, Kankakee, IL
17. Fontbonne College, St. Louis, MO
18. Shorter College, Rome, GA
19. Thomas More College, Crestview Hills, KY
20. Montreat-Anderson College, Montreat, NC
21. Belhaven College, Jackson, MS
22. Albertus Magnus College, New Haven, CT
23. Ohio Dominican College, Columbus, OH
24. William Penn College, Des Moines, IA

Today, these twenty-four institutions operate some fifty learning centers and enroll over 26,000 working adult students which, together with the 30,000 students enrolled at the University of Phoenix, constitute the major portion of students enrolled in programs created exclusively for working adults.

The University of Phoenix model of the Adult-Centered University was the original model for most of the adult-centered programs in U.S. higher education. Therefore, it seems reasonable to us that we use the University of Phoenix as the exemplar of this model.

There remains the issue of why we believe that it is not self-serving to recommend a for-profit corporate structure. We believe this for several reasons. The University of Phoenix is at least as educationally effective as other institutions using some form of the UOP Model. Certainly, in terms of taxpayer support, it is the most cost effective. UOP's educational effectiveness is measured every day by what we believe to be the most sophisticated quality management and outcomes measurement system in use in higher education. We do not believe it would have been possible to develop the system—or to maintain and enhance it these many years—were it not for a corporate structure that encourages innovation and the discipline which our bottom-line (read *for-profit*) responsibilities demand.

We could not operate the University of Phoenix at a profit if we did not place our customers (students) first or if we failed to meet the academic competition presented by tax-subsidized institutions. With public and private universities deriving well over 60 percent of their operating expenses from direct and indirect public subsidy, the University of Phoenix has managed to secure market share and make a profit wherever it operates—and it has done so with no public subsidy. The for-profit model requires the lowest level of taxpayer support of any of the models we have examined, whether they are traditional or non-traditional.

We hope that readers will judge this position paper on the merit of its arguments and on the vision for higher education that it sets forth.

One of the few areas in which most economists agree is that a nation's human capital and the new ideas and innovations generated by that human capital constitute a major engine of economic growth. Now that the fastest-growing part of the American economy is neither manufacturing nor traditional services, but the knowledge-sector of the service industry, investments in human capital, particularly in the form of higher education, pay extra dividends. The economic returns from education are both social and personal. They are social in that the benefits of an individual's education extend to other workers and are diffused throughout society. For individuals, as the data conclusively show, there is a direct and powerful correlation between higher education and higher incomes. Even here, there is a social benefit—the higher one's income, the higher one's taxes and the greater one's contribution to the support of social services.

The American standard of living, the productivity of the American economy and America's ability to compete in the global economy no longer rest exclusively, or even primarily, on natural resources, capital plant, access to financial capital, or population. These assets are now secondary to the quality of human capital in determining a nation's economic condition and standard of living. Every industrial nation now has equal access to raw materials; capital plants can be located anywhere in the world; financial capital moves quickly to wherever the returns are highest; and the brute labor of a large population can only compete with brute labor anywhere in the world. The critical competitive advantage that any nation enjoys is now the quality of its human capital. This quality is largely determined by education.

Human capital resides in both individuals and organizations. In individuals, it is their knowledge and skills and how, through their intelligence, creativity, and energy, they apply their knowledge and skills to the improvement of the economy. Organizational or collective human capital resides in groups of all kinds: corporations, government organizations, universities, and so on. It is obviously present in groups of scientists who work together on a problem; it is present in a team of engineers, production specialists, and marketers who work to develop a new product; it is present, to some degree, in almost every group engaged in a common task. Innovations in the form of new scientific concepts, new products, new ways to organize production, and new ways to market and sell goods and services provide the main stimulus for economic growth. Of course, for these innovations to stimulate growth, the products flowing from them must be produced by companies with a workforce capable of developing, producing, and marketing them efficiently and with a level of quality that meets the expectations of the consumer.

Although innovations come from many sources, most of them are produced by our college-educated workers. The contributions of innovators such as Steve Jobs and Bill Gates notwithstanding, almost all scientific and technical innovations are produced by college-trained scientists and engineers, and most other innovations are produced by college-educated managers and professionals, usually working as members of a team. Not only do the college-educated workers, about 25 percent of the workforce, produce most of the innovations, they also make the decisions that determine the level of knowledge and skills possessed by the other 75 percent.

The Economic Lever of Higher Education

For all workers, of whatever occupation and rank, the world of work is no longer a secure place. Employers can no longer hold out the expectation of permanent employment, since survival for most firms depends upon rapid responses to changing markets and this often entails the laying off of employees. Workers face the challenge of up to seven to ten major career changes in a working lifetime. Today, a worker's security depends upon maintaining the knowledge and skills that all employers find desirable.

Each occupational change requires a different mix of knowledge and skills, usually of increasing complexity. If one expects to prosper with a rising career, worklife-long education is an economic imperative. Without it, one's career is likely to stagnate, which soon translates into a real decline in living standards. The recent recession that saw the layoff, followed by long periods of unemployment, of tens of thousands of well-educated middle managers and professionals whose repertoire of skills had narrowed to specific jobs is a cautionary tale that should not be ignored. Many of these layoffs arose from the declining cost of capital goods versus labor. Between 1987 and 1990, the index of capital costs rose from 100 to 110, while the index of labor costs rose to 130. Under these circumstances it behooves anyone who hopes for regular employment to gain and maintain the skills needed to add value to production processes based on sophisticated information systems and production machinery.

Although the present may look bleak to many college-trained workers who have lost their jobs, the Bureau of Labor Statistics projects that 41 percent of all job growth to the year 2005 will require managerial, technical, and professional college graduates. The largest number of these jobs will be executives and managers in marketing, public relations, advertising, communications, and labor relations; technical jobs in engineering, communications, and computers; and professional jobs in health sciences and the law.

Income and Enfranchisement

In 1994, only 64 percent of recent high school graduates who were not enrolled in a postsecondary institution were employed; for recent high school dropouts, the situation was even worse: only 43 percent of recent high school dropouts had employment. Those who did find jobs could expect an average entry level wage of $12,500 rising to $16,000 as experienced workers. Furthermore, the lower the wage, the lower the probability the employer will provide health care benefits. Too often a high school diploma has become a one-way ticket into the ranks of the working poor. The economic rewards of a high school diploma are in stark contrast to the economic rewards of a bachelor's degree, whose bearer will receive, on average, an entry-level salary of $23,000 with no ceiling if the bearer is talented and lucky.[1] University graduates are the only group whose members can reasonably expect to have short periods of unemployment and manage to achieve the American dream of earning more than their parents and offering their children the same opportunity.

The earnings benefits of higher education for all ethnic groups and both sexes is compelling; for minorities this benefit is truly the avenue of opportunity. Based on 1992 data, a person with some college education will only earn 15 percent more than he or she would as a high school graduate. Completing the degree raises that percentage to 47 percent for a white male and an astonishing 109 percent for a black female. Figure 1.1 shows the education-based earnings advantage for black, hispanic and white men and women.

Higher education is the *sine qua non* of the good life for nations and for individuals. Consider that:

- In 1980, 25- to 34-year-old white male college graduates earned 16 percent

FIGURE 1.1
Mean Weekly Earnings, by Race, Gender, and Education Level

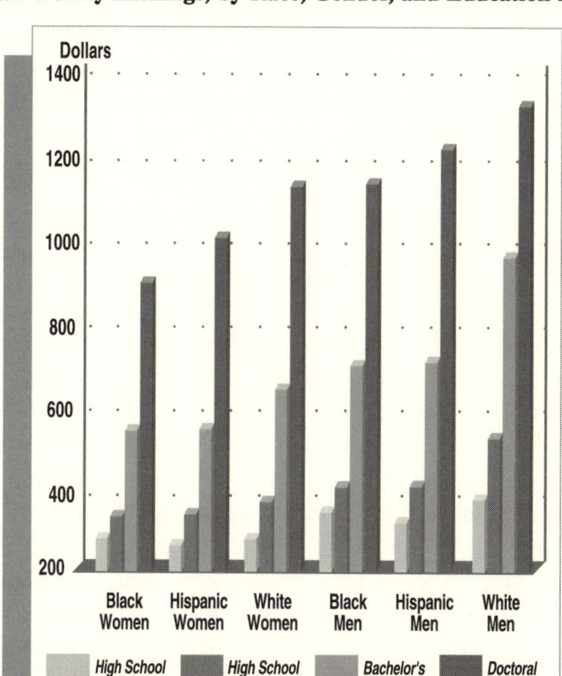

Source: U.S. Department of Labor, Bureau of Labor Statistics

more than their high school graduate counterparts and 39 percent more than those who did not complete high school;

- In 1994, 25- to 34-year-old college graduates were earning 52 percent more than their high school graduate counterparts, and 84 percent more than those who did not complete high school; and
- In 1994, 2.9 percent of university graduates were unemployed versus 6.7 percent of high school graduates, and 12.6 percent of high school dropouts.

The disparity in the economic status of high school dropouts or graduates and those with a college education is not healthy in any sense for American society since, ultimately, these disparities can only lead to what Benjamin Disraeli described in England in the mid-nineteenth century: "The rich and the poor: Two nations; between whom there is no intercourse and no sympathy; who are as ignorant of each other's habits, thoughts and feelings, as if they were dwellers in different zones, or inhabitants of different planets." Today, much the same is true in America. We can amend Disraeli's characterization to read: "Two nations: One well-educated, affluent, and involved; the other, ignorant, poor and passive"—and the gap is widening. For example:

- In the 1964 presidential election, 25- to 34-year-old college graduates were 14 percent more likely to vote than their high school graduate counterparts, and 34 percent more likely to vote than those who did not complete high school; and
- By the 1992 presidential election, 25- to 34-year-old college graduates were 58 percent more likely to vote than their high school graduate counterparts, and twice as likely to vote than those who did not complete high school.

Summary

Higher education is more important than ever before and will only become more so as greater knowledge and skills are required by a growing number of individuals to function effectively in the increasingly knowledge-driven economy. As this paper will show, the most efficient way to address the issue of increased need for higher education for the workforce is through the development of for-profit adult-centered universities.

Note

1. Based on the field of study, women graduates earned from $18,000 to $30,000 with an average of $20,500. Men earned from $18,900 to $30,900 with an average of $23,900. (See American Council on Education, *Research Briefs*, vol. 5, no. 2, 1994.)

2

Costs and Access in Higher Education

Higher Education and Budgetary Constraints

The impact of federal and state budgetary constraints on higher education affects both public and private institutions. Reduced federal funding has forced some retrenchment, especially on research universities, but the greatest impact has been on public institutions as they have had to compete for scarce state tax dollars with the demands of welfare, health care, criminal justice, and housing a burgeoning prison population. To a lesser extent, declining state support has also affected private institutions since most receive two to three percent of their budgets from their home states.

The division of support for higher education between the federal and state governments shows how the burden of higher education has shifted to the states. In 1960, the federal government assumed 16 percent of the financial burden for postsecondary education and the states assumed 19 percent. In 1990, the federal share was down to 11 percent and the state share increased to 23 percent. Until recently this gap continued to widen. Figure 2.1 shows the relative decline in state support of higher education.

This decline is one reason that public institutions have raised fees and tuition and reduced program offerings. Not only has this priced many students, especially those from minority communities, out of the public education market, it has forced colleges and universities to deny entry to tens of thousands of qualified high school graduates.

Financial Constraints on Access to Higher Education

The cost to the nation for higher education has far outpaced the consumer price index (CPI). Between 1981 and 1991, the CPI rose by 50

FIGURE 2.1
Federal and State Support for Higher Education

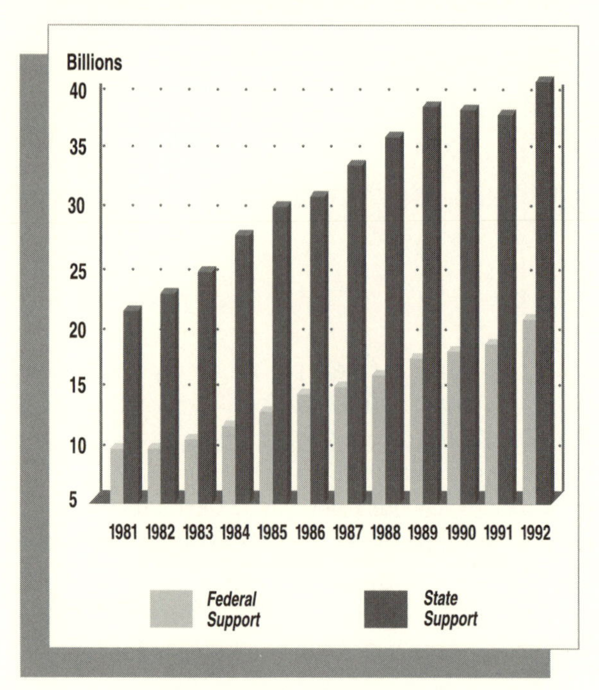

Source: U.S. Department of Education, National Center for Education Statistics

percent, but even conservative estimates of the costs of higher education show an increase of 88 to 110 percent over the same period. It is data like these that caused the American Council on Education to predict in 1992 that, if this trend is not stopped, a student entering a public college ten years from now will pay $75,000 in tuition alone for a bachelor's degree. Increases in the cost of attending college reflect more than general inflation in consumer prices. As figure 2.2 shows, the three fastest growing costs during the 1980s were tuition for public colleges and universities, medical care, and tuition for private colleges and universities.

Although the rate of tuition increase after 1991 was projected to decline, the 1995 College Board Annual Survey of Colleges showed that tuition and fees for undergraduates at American four-year colleges were still projected to increase approximately six percent in 1995, as they had

FIGURE 2.2
Increase in Higher Education Costs Compared to Consumer Purchases and Median Family Income, 1980–1990

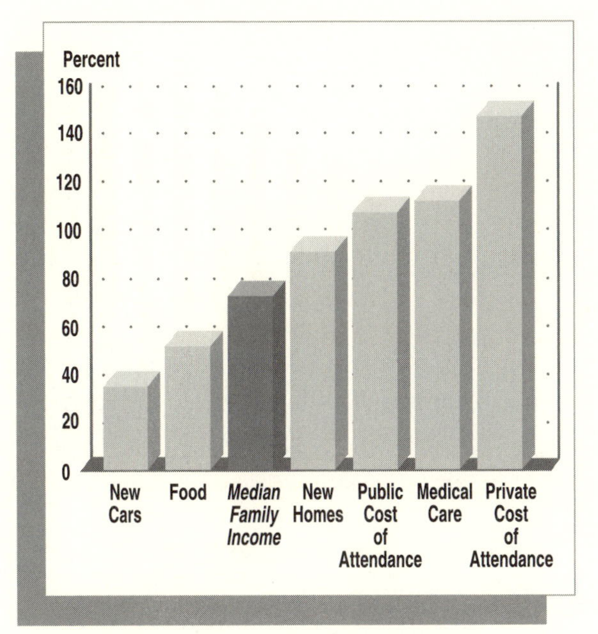

Source: National Commission on Responsibilities for Financing Postsecondary Education

in the previous three years. Overall, growth in costs still exceeds the CPI and the burden of its dramatic increase in the 1980s is still borne by today's consumers of higher education.

As traditional colleges and universities strive to meet the needs of an increasingly ethnically and racially diverse student population and continue their commitments to research and public service, both public and private colleges and universities have had to raise their tuition so high that they have now priced virtually all lower income families out of the higher education market. Paying for college now ranks second to buying a home as the most expensive investment for the average family. Figure 2.3 shows that tuition costs have skyrocketed over the last decade in relation to personal savings.

FIGURE 2.3
Average Higher Education Tuition and Fees Compared to Personal Savings for Blacks and Whites

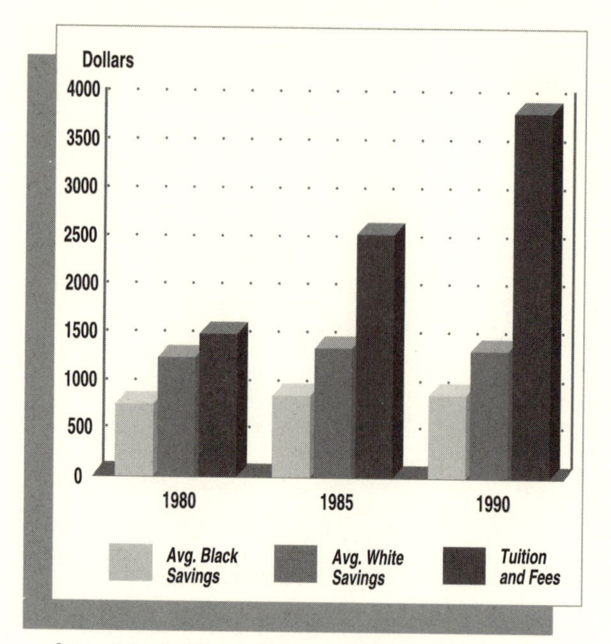

Source: University of Phoenix, Department of Institutional Research Based on 1992 Statistical Abstract of the United States and U.S. Department of Education, National Center for Education Statistics Data

As figure 2.4 shows, the costs of a college education require a share of family income that is growing for all segments of the middle class. By 1990, for families whose earnings place them at the 25th percentile of the income distribution, private schools are completely out of reach and the annual costs of education at public schools exceed their personal savings by a factor of five. For families at the 50th percentile of the income distribution, the annual cost of public education exceeds their personal savings by a factor of three. The problem of financial access to higher education is not ameliorated until one's family income reaches the 75th percentile.

It is unlikely that tuition increases will fall within the CPI as state legislatures implement "flip-flop" plans to decrease state support while

FIGURE 2.4
Annual Per Student Cost of Higher Education as a Percent of Family Income for Families Falling in the 25th and 50th Percentiles of the Income Distribution

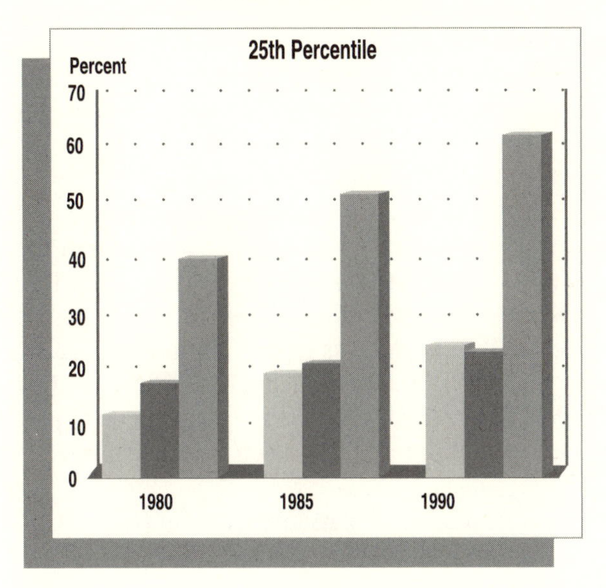

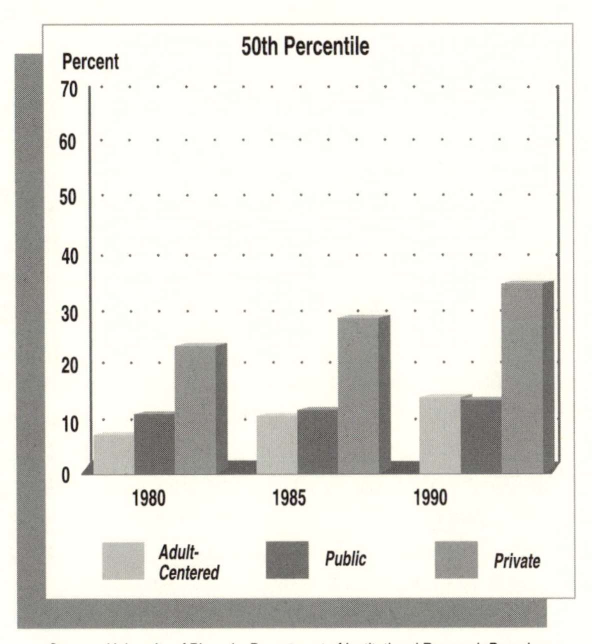

Source: University of Phoenix, Department of Institutional Research Based on U.S. Department of Education, National Center for Education Statistics Data

increasing both tuition and financial aid. The assumption under plans of this kind is that revenue from students able to pay full tuition will fund the additional expense of financial aid for students who are not able to pay their way. This assumption will hold in a few of the nation's most prestigious institutions but, overall, it is not financially sound. In all but a few select institutions, the number of students requiring financial assistance will almost always outnumber those capable of paying full tuition. The result: access to higher education for the lower and middle class is restricted even further.

The relationship between the level of family income and college attendance is evident in enrollment data. While 67 percent of high socioeconomic status middle achievers in high school attend college, only 43 percent of low socioeconomic status middle achievers do so. In 1979 a student whose family income was in the top quartile had a four times greater chance of earning a bachelor's degree by the age of twenty-four than did a student whose family income was in the lowest quartile. Today the well-off student's chances are nineteen times greater.[1]

Financial and Educational Costs of Growth: The California Example

Tuition and fees at the University of California increased 155 percent between 1989 and 1993. In the California State University system, they increased 120 percent between 1990 and 1993. Community colleges have shown similar or greater increases. State support of higher education has decreased, which has occasioned layoffs of part-time and nontenured faculty and the cancellation of thousands of classes. For 1995–96 enrollees in the California State University system, program cuts are taking a substantial toll; the system chancellor has stated that the current average of six years that it takes to earn a four-year bachelor's degree will henceforth be eight years.

Rising tuition and reduced capacity have closed the doors to tens of thousands of qualified students, especially to minorities who can least afford the increased costs. Between the fall of 1992 and 1993, community college enrollments dropped by 137,000 students, California State University enrollments dropped by 22,000 students, and University of California enrollments dropped by 3,000 students; 1994–1995 data show continued declines.[2] As an example, community colleges lost an additional

38,000 students between 1993 and 1995. The experiences of California are being played out in a less extreme fashion in several other states today and there are real prospects that the list of states no longer able to afford their higher education systems will grow in the coming years.

Education for the Academic Elite

In 1995 taxpayers paid just over $3 billion to underwrite the education of the 161,000 talented undergraduates attending our nation's fifty most expensive private colleges and universities. Next year they will pay even more. This nearly invisible public subsidy of the private schools comes in many forms, as is illustrated in table 2.1 below by 1993 data from Swarthmore College.[3]

TABLE 2.1
1993 Taxpayer Subsidy and Forgone Taxation to Support Swarthmore Undergraduate Education[4]

Category of Expense	Per-Student Dollar Amount (per Annum)	Mechanism of Taxpayer Subsidy	Dollar Value of Subsidy
Endowments, Gifts, etc.[5]	$23,000	Those who endow and/or otherwise provide financial support to the College receive tax consideration.	$9,660
Direct Government Support	$4,000	The federal and state governments provide direct subsidy for the College's activities.	$4,000
Forgone Property Tax	$230,769	Public and private not-for-profit institutions generally do not pay property tax.	$3,462
Forgone Sales Tax	$8,800	Public and private not-for-profit institutions generally do not pay sales tax.	$572
Student Tuition and Fees	$17,640	For comparable tuition revenue, a for-profit institution would earn a pre-tax profit of $1,357 and would pay 50 percent federal, state and local taxes on this amount.	$1,591[6]
Per-Student Annual Taxpayer Subsidy			$19,285

No doubt every society needs to educate an intellectual elite and, in ten to twenty years, many graduates of these elites schools will have become productive members of society, returning perhaps more economic value than they took in public subsidy. However, it is just as important to invest in the education of our current workforce. Were 161,000 nonprivileged students to attend for-profit adult-centered universities, as this study will prove, taxpayers would receive a modest $16.26 million annually in tax benefits.

Higher Education's Phantom Contribution to America's Balance of Trade

A frequently mentioned offset to the cost of maintaining the American university system is its positive balance of trade in the global market of higher education, but there is less here than meets the eye. Foreign students enrolled in U.S. institutions of higher education bring $4 billion in foreign exchange to the U.S., thus providing the basis of higher education's claim that it joins a select few U.S. industries, such as aerospace, that have a multibillion dollar positive foreign trade balance. Yet these claims may not run deep. Tuition and fees account for 16 percent of the total costs for public colleges and universities, and 39 percent of the costs for private institutions. Other than revenue generated by the institution, the remainder of the costs are borne by tax-based subsidies and funds from endowments and gifts; these tax benefits flow to all students whether citizens or foreigners.

No one knows exactly how much it costs the American taxpayer to realize the $4 billion derived from the tuition, fees, board and room paid by foreign students. However, $4 billion represents only 2.5 percent of the higher education budget, while 3 percent of the seats in America's colleges and universities are occupied by foreign students. A much higher percentage of seats are occupied by foreign students in the more costly and labor-intensive graduate programs of America's universities. For example, in 1989 about 25 percent of all students enrolled in graduate science and engineering programs were non-U.S. citizens; in engineering and mathematics, over 55 percent of those receiving a Ph.D. degree were foreign students.[7] Given these statistics, it is likely that the taxpayer is paying considerably more than $4 billion to earn the $4 billion tuition paid by foreign students. In short, America is selling its higher education services at less than cost and that cost will be recovered only to the extent these foreign students remain in the U.S. and apply their talents to improving the American economy.

Low Productivity and High Costs in Traditional Institutions

One of the reasons why the cost of higher education has outrun the rate of inflation is the low rate of productivity increase in traditional colleges and universities. The average increase in the cost of all services peaked in early 1981 at 6.2 percent above inflation and has now fallen to 3.2 percent above inflation. However, if one removes medical care, transportation, and education, productivity increases in other services have dropped price increases to just 2.5 percent over inflation.[8] This contrasts sharply with the price increases found in higher education. The massive increases in the cost of a college education experienced during the 1980s are by no means behind us. In 1991 the increase in the cost of tuition and fees at four-year undergraduate institutions was 190 percent greater than the increase in the consumer price index (CPI); in 1992, the increase was 262 percent greater than the CPI increase; and in 1993, the increase was 154 percent more than the CPI increase. Although the rate of increase has slowed, it will still exceed the CPI in the 1995–96 academic year. A brief look at how traditional colleges and universities operate explains why.

Facilities at traditional colleges and universities are severely underutilized for much of the year. Campuses are shut down for two to four weeks around the new year and for another week break for spring vacation. In most institutions, the school year ends in late May or early June and the new academic year does not begin until after Labor Day. In all, facilities are largely unused or underused for over four months a year. There is little flexibility in the assignment of faculty in traditional institutions. A doctorate is required for most positions, doctoral-prepared instructors are usually trained in narrow fields of study, and such instructors are only effective in that narrow field whatever the level of demand for the courses they teach.

Education of Youth—Slow Return on High Investment

As vital to our long-term welfare as preschool, primary, secondary, and postsecondary education are, it is still a fact that an investment in preschoolers will not lead to higher productivity for twenty-five to thirty years; for elementary students the waiting period will be twenty to twenty-five years; for high school students it will be ten to fifteen years; and for traditional university students it will still be five years or more before they are in a position to affect the quality of the workforce. On the other hand, educating those already in the workforce has both immediate and long-term benefits.

In 1995 a computer citation search for professional articles on higher education was conducted. It was found that 8.5 percent of the articles mentioned adult education. A previous search of articles appearing in *The Chronicle of Higher Education* revealed that less than 10 percent addressed adult-centered higher education. Similarly, there is no mention of higher education for working adults in *Mandate for Change*, the Clinton administration's agenda prepared by the Progressive Policy Institute; President Clinton's January 1994 speech on educational reform, given before the American Council on Education, devoted one sentence to the education of working adults.[9] At this time, 50 percent of students are over the age of 22 and our best estimate is that 80 percent of them are working in career or career-aspiring positions.

Approximately 90 percent of the total education budget is directed at K-12 and youth-centered higher education, where its economic returns lie five to twenty-five years in the future. While this is probably as it should be, would it not be wise policy to multiply the impact of the 10 percent allocated to adult education by facilitating the development of for-profit, adult-centered universities that pay more in taxes than they receive in tax subsidies?

Need for New Institutions of Higher Education

Meeting the higher education needs of the nontraditional working adult student will require new nontraditional institutions that are flexible, are able to apply new technologies, are willing to provide access to all who need it, are cost effective and that place no burden on the taxpayer. In our opinion, the institution best suited for the task of educating the American workforce is the for-profit adult-centered university.

Notes

1. See "Cost of 4-Year Degree Passes $100,000 Mark," *New York Times*, May 4, 1994, quoting Iowa City higher education policy analyst Thomas G. Mortenson,

who asserts that higher education costs are being shifted from the taxpayers to the students and their families: "We're heading toward a price-based admissions policy where people who can afford it will go to college and others won't."

The erosion of the value of the G.I. Bill provides dramatic evidence of the growing cost of education relative to the ability of students to pay for it. In 1940, the G.I. Bill provided $50 a month for a single veteran and fifty years later that figure is now $400. However, the value of $50 in 1940 dollars is now $2,107. (See, "50 Years Later, the Value of the G.I. Bill is Questioned," *New York Times*, June 22, 1994.)

2. "California Higher Education Enrollments Plunge," *Cross Talk*, January 1994, California Higher Education Policy Center.
3. See "One Top College's Price Tag: Why So Low and So High?" *New York Times*, July 27, 1994.
4. The true level of taxpayer subsidy is almost certainly higher than reflected in the table 2.1 because the potential tax value of the college's land and the interest on its endowments are not known.
5. Since other values in this column are known, the amount allocated to endowments, etc., were adjusted to match the total expenses, as stated by Swarthmore. However, Swarthmore also states that endowments, alumni contributions and gifts account for more than 50 percent of the institution's funding. There is no explanation for the disparity.
6. While a forgone opportunity for taxation is not the same as a direct subsidy by the taxpayer, this figure does reflect the tax revenue to be realized in a for-profit institution.
7. "Commission on the Future of Worker-Management Relations, Fact Finding Report, May 1994," p.13, U. S. Departments of Labor and Commerce.
8. "Costs Drop as Productivity Improves," *Wall Street Journal*, July 18, 1994.
9. Indicative of official ignorance of the importance of adult higher education is the response of Secretary of Labor Robert Reich, who, when asked his opinion of the DeVry Institute, which enrolls 15,000 adults largely in technical programs, replied that he had never heard of it. (See *Washington Post*, July 2, 1995, "It's Elementary: Buy Education Stocks Now.")

3

Adult-Centered Universities: Education for the American Workforce

Six Distinct Higher Education Student Populations

Over the past two decades, the student population has become more diverse in age and educational purpose.[1] To better understand the needs of working adult students in relation to the institutional systems that might meet those needs, it is necessary to have a clear picture of the diversity of the student population. Today, six distinct student groups make up most college and university populations.[2] The six groups and their approximate student populations are:

- **Group 1:** *3.9 million traditional undergraduate students*—ages 17 to 24, seeking a bachelor's degree and enrolled full-time at a campus;
- **Group 2:** *650,000 traditional graduate students*—ages 22 to 34, seeking either an academic or professional master's or doctoral degree and enrolled full-time at a campus;
- **Group 3:** *2.9 million semi-traditional undergraduate students*—ages 17 to 24, seeking a bachelor's degree and enrolled part-time at a campus, usually working part-time in an entry-level job;
- **Group 4:** *487,000 semi-traditional graduate students*—ages 22 to 34, seeking an academic master's or doctoral degree and enrolled part-time at a campus. (Employment varies among this population. Some have part-time work in a variety of campus and off-campus jobs and others work in full-time careers, e.g., school teachers, principals and superintendents or college teachers completing their doctoral degree.);
- **Group 5:** *5.3 million non-traditional undergraduate students*—ages 25 and up, they are career-oriented members of the labor force; usually seeking a first degree in an on-campus or off-campus program, enrolled full- or part-time and career-oriented members of the labor force; and

- **Group 6:** *880,000 non-traditional graduate students*—ages 25 and up, working full-time in a chosen career, enrolled full- or part-time, seeking a professional master's or doctoral degree in an on-campus or off-campus program and working full-time in a chosen career.

Figure 3.1 shows the approximate distribution of the nation's 1994 population of students enrolled in colleges and universities. Traditional-age undergraduate students (Groups 1–4) are those typically thought of as the consumers of higher education; however, they constitute only 56 percent of the higher education student population. The remaining 44 percent (Groups 5–6) are the adults whose numbers are growing and who, by the 21st century, will constitute half of the higher education student population. Most importantly, of these more than 6 million adults, some 80 percent are working and most work full-time.

Groups 1–4 are served by "traditional" colleges and universities, that is, institutions with a tenured, full-time faculty, a comprehensively equipped main campus and, in most cases, student residential facilities. These institutions provide the desired educational services and have adequate capacity to meet the needs of traditional students for the foreseeable future. However, they do not provide many of the educational services needed by working adult students, nor do they have the capacity needed to accommodate this growing segment of the student population, which is projected to increase through the year 2005.

Defining Educational Characteristics of the Adult-Centered University

The adult-centered university is educationally effective and efficient and is designed to serve the needs of most semitraditional graduate students and nontraditional undergraduate and graduate students (Groups 4, 5, and 6).

Our experience, and over a decade's worth of evaluative data derived from that experience, shows that the optimum learning environment for working adults is one that is structured for the efficient use of the limited time available to them. We have found that adults perform best using a curriculum with specific learning outcomes delivered by working professionals who are knowledgeable in both the theory and practice of their subject area and who have received training in instructing working adult students. The goal of this system is to enable the students to achieve a

FIGURE 3.1
Estimated 1994 Enrollment in Higher Education by Education Function

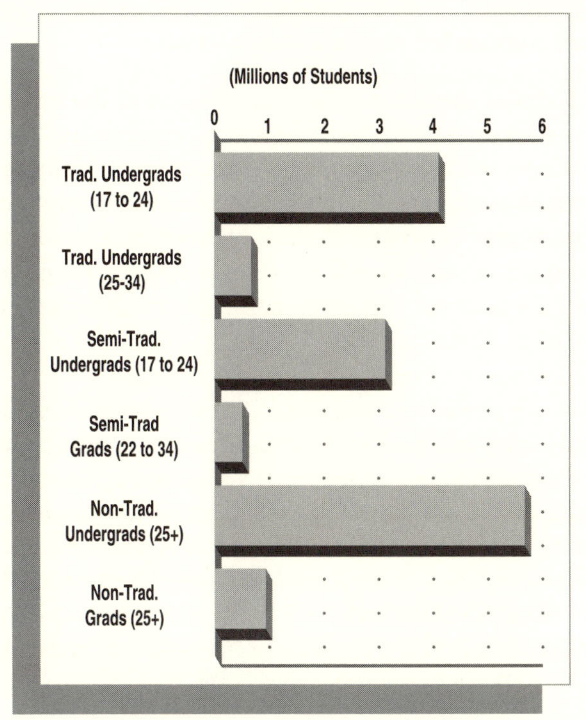

Source: University of Phoenix, Department of Institutional Research Based on U.S. Department of Education, National Center for Education Statistics Data

given set of learning outcomes in the most efficient way possible. Following are the educational characteristics of a well-designed adult-centered university*:

- The professionally developed curriculum is standardized for all courses being taught in all locations by all instructors and facilitates the learning that occurs from instructor to students and among students. The curriculum has specified learning outcomes and standardized evaluation instruments. It gives balanced consideration to theory and practice, and requires the student to apply in the workplace what has been learned in the classroom and to bring to the classroom what has been learned in the workplace.

---

* See Appendix A for a more complete discussion of the adult-centered teaching/learning model.

- The educational structure requires students to work in groups where they learn and practice the skills of leadership and team membership and the values of cooperation and conciliation that they can bring to their own places of employment.
- The faculty consists of academically qualified working professionals who can bring the professional and practical realities of the workplace into the classroom, and who have the ability to relate to and communicate with adult students within the context of small, intense learning groups.
- There is a training program for the faculty members that enables them to be effective in delivering instruction faithful to the curriculum.
- Instruction is time-efficient and offered at times and places convenient to the students, with compressed classes usually scheduled in the evenings or on weekends at learning centers that, whenever possible, are only a brief commute from work or home and are near safe parking or public transportation.
- The organizational structure and practice maintain a constructive tension between financial and academic accountability in which faculty debate and determine academic policies and procedures within the financial constraints of a budget approved by management.
- The quality management system measures the performance of students, faculty and administrative staff against standards that have been validated by the requirements of the workplace, and makes continuous improvement possible in the teaching/learning environment.
- The degree, through its recognition by employers, is portable across work environments. This portability is due to having learning outcomes that focus on knowledge, values and skills that are essential to the workplace, and because the institution is able to demonstrate students' achievement of these skills to employers.
- The institution's management embraces the student as an intelligent and informed consumer of educational services and seeks constantly to improve the efficiency and quality of those services. Each learning group has direct access to management through its student representatives.

Access and Educational Efficiency

Adult-centered institutions offer a level of access and a level of educational efficiency that traditional colleges and universities cannot match. Data published by the American Council on Education help to explain why so few working adults ever earn a degree or, if they do, why it takes so long. At the community college level, only 20 percent of adult students attend full-time; this rises to 50 percent for undergraduate students at four-year public colleges and universities but drops back to 35 percent for graduate students.[3] Our own data show that a large number of those who attend adult-centered programs, where working students can attend as full-time students, are enrolled to take advantage of an efficient means of completing their degrees. These data also show that a large number of those who attend the University of Phoenix have been unable to complete their degrees at the traditional institutions they have attended and are enrolled to take advantage of an efficient means of completing degrees they may have worked on for years.[4]

Most full-time workers who now attend colleges and universities are young managers and professionals. In our opinion, adult-centered universities can serve their needs more efficiently than can traditional institutions, but, more importantly, they can serve the needs of those millions of adults who have, for whatever reason, been unable to begin or to complete the higher education they need to enter into professional ranks. These degree completion and first-time students come from all occupations and ranks, but they are primarily from the ranks of middle and lower management, supervisors, technicians, specialists, and, to a lesser extent, the most ambitious of the front-line production and service workers. Providing access to higher education for production and service workers answers one of the criticisms of programs merely designed to train these workers for high skills: "You can train the workers but where are the high-skills jobs?" In contrast to job training, higher education provides workers with a broad repertoire of skills that qualifies them for a greatly increased number and variety of technical and professional positions and, in many instances, gives them the vision and motivation to create new jobs within their companies or to start new companies to fulfill their vision.[5]

This is especially important to minority men and women who have had to skip college after high school. Often the only access to the professions for this group is a degree from an adult-centered university. Among 1980 high school seniors whose family incomes were in the lowest quartile, only 7.7 percent of blacks and 4.9 percent of Hispanics had attained a bachelor's degree by 1986. In 1989, among people aged 25 years and older, 20 percent of whites had completed college versus 11.1 percent of blacks and 8.5 percent of Hispanics.[6] While audited national data for six-year baccalaureate graduation rate by race and ethnicity for all students are not available, the combined average six-year graduation rates for Arizona, California and New Mexico (unaudited) are 39 percent for whites, 31 percent for Hispanics and 20 percent for blacks.[7] The graduation rate in historically black colleges is estimated to be 45 percent.[8] As low as these graduation rates appear, they are expected to drop further as working adult students of large public colleges and universities in the 1990s find that it will take them up to eight years of attendance to secure all of the courses required to earn a degree. In contrast, the five-year graduation rate in the adult-centered programs we have studied is 63 percent for whites, 53 percent for Hispanics and 50 percent for blacks.

As figure 3.2 suggests, adult-centered programs would appear to be a far more effective method of raising the graduation rate for minorities than are the commonly required courses in racial and ethnic sensitivity and the costly retention programs found at most colleges and universities. The reason is simple. In adult-centered programs, students are working adults who have established satisfactory workplace relationships and who have well-formed interpersonal support groups (e.g., family and professional) and who share the same educational goal: earning their degrees in the most efficient manner possible so they can improve their career opportunities and incomes.[9]

Critics may object that these claims about minority graduation rates represent unfounded comparisons. We recognize the validity of this criticism: working adult blacks, for example, represent only a subset of the black student graduation statistics. However, until graduation rates are depoliticized and acquire a finer structure that permits needed distinctions among groups, there is no way to determine the extent to which this point is valid.

The best way for America to compete successfully in a global economy of increasing technical complexity and sophistication is to move more and more workers of both genders and all ethnic groups into the ranks of technical and professional knowledge workers.

Participation Rates in Employer Subsidized Programs

Taken together with the abundant evidence of need for workforce education, the low rate at which American workers participate in employer subsidized educational programs is one indication of the inability of traditional institutions to provide the needed worker education. In 1993, Hewitt Associates, an international firm specializing in the administration of employee benefit and compensation programs, surveyed 858 U.S.

FIGURE 3.2
Baccaulaureate Graduation Rates by Race/Ethnicity and Type of Institution

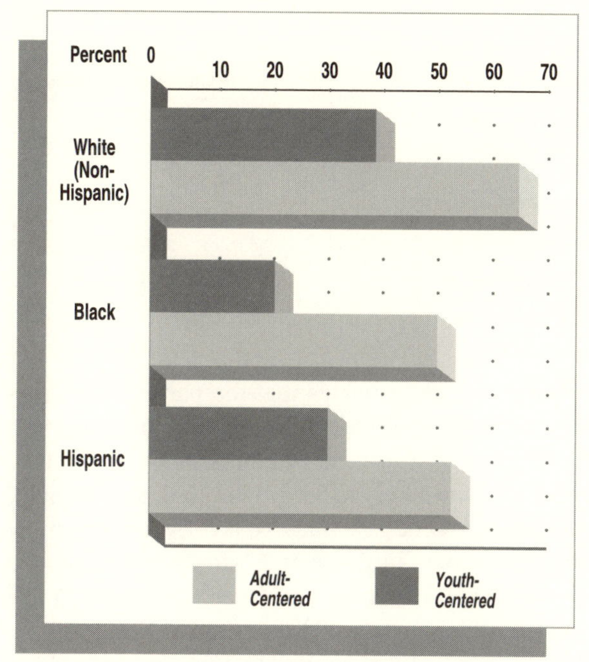

Source: University of Phoenix, Department of Institutional Research

employers known to provide education to employees. The purpose of the survey was to determine the pattern and level of participation of employees in employer-sponsored educational programs.[10] The survey covered the types of expenses and courses, dollar limits on reimbursement, eligibility of full- and part-time employees and participation rates.[11] Among the 651 employers who responded to this section of the survey, 42 percent place no dollar limit on the amount of tuition they will reimburse, and another 25 percent provide from $2,000 to more than $5,000 in tuition assistance; only 12 percent provide $1,500 or less.

In contrast to what can be described as generous employer support of employee education, the median rate at which employees enrolled in educational programs supported by their employers was only 6.5 percent, and the maximum participation rate was 19 percent. Most of the employees who do participate are managers or other professionals and most

TABLE 3.1
Proportion of Medium-to-Large Employers Reimbursing Employee Tuition Expenses at 50 percent or Greater

Percent of tuition expenses reimbursed	Percent of responding employers
50 percent or greater	70 percent
75 percent or greater	67 percent
80 percent or greater	59 percent
90 percent or greater	55 percent
100 percent	52 percent

of them are young, which indicates that the participation rate is abysmally low among lower ranked employees and those thirty years and older, just the groups most in need of educational renewal. Given that older employees are most likely to be laid off, their low participation rate is disturbing. For example, despite massive layoffs at New England banks, the number of participants in Bank of Boston's educational assistance program is an anemic 500 out of a workforce of 14,000. At Cleveland's American Greetings Corp., only 481 out of a workforce of 21,100 participated. With the insecurity generated by massive downsizing and the general understanding among workers that education is the best safety net, employee apathy can hardly be the sole explanation for the low participation rates.

Of the hypotheses that might help to explain the low participation rates, two seem especially plausible. First, the times, locations, and educational networks available through traditional institutions neither meet the educational needs of the employees nor accommodate the constraints presented by their discretionary time and schedules. Second, there is insufficient information as to what programs are available.

In our opinion, the most practical way to bring a significant increase in the rate of participation is through a vigorous recruiting effort by institutions designed to serve the adult market. This requires effective marketing and advertising backed up by knowledgeable enrollment counselors who are capable of explaining the importance of higher education to an employee's economic survival and who are rewarded for their success in enrolling students.[12]

The New Worker-Management Compact

The emergence of the global economy has transformed the structure of the American economy and the organization of the American corporation. This transformation has radically altered the relationship between employer and employee. The globalization of most markets has, among other things, resulted in company downsizing, reengineering for flexibility, and the rise of the virtual corporation. Because of these changes, few companies now hold out the prospect of lifelong employment and few employees expect it. With traditional bonds of loyalty undergoing reexamination and change, a new worker-management compact is now gaining popularity. In this compact, employees give their best to the company as long as they are employed, and companies provide employees with the opportunity to move from job to job within the company and with ongoing career development education and training. If the compact is successful, employees, at date of termination, will be better qualified for their next job than they were when they went to work for the company.[13]

To make such a compact effective requires more than the commitment of companies and employees. It also requires institutional structures both within and outside the company to make it a reality. Within the company there must be the possibility of constant upgrading of company-specific skills, and outside the company there must be institutions able to provide the non-company-specific, generalized education and skill training the employee will need for the next job. As the Hewitt study suggests, institutions able to provide generalized education and skill training are not currently accessible to millions of workers. Until such institutions are widely available, the new worker-management compact will not materialize and worker-management relations will become even more contentious than they are now. The cost will be lower productivity in the American economy and lower living standards for the American people.[14]

Clearly, adult-centered programs can provide many of the educational and training services the new compact requires, and they are certainly capable of dramatically increasing the rate at which employees participate in tuition assistance programs. First, they are committed to serving the perceived needs of the companies—employers and employees—in their market areas. Second, if their marketing and advertising campaigns are aggressive, it almost ensures that most of the employers and employees in their market areas are aware of the programs they offer. Third, most programs have widely distributed marketing materials—ads, brochures, and studies—that stress the importance of higher education to both employers and employees. Fourth, their enrollment counselors are knowledgeable and effective in counseling prospective students.

The Emergence of the Contingent Worker

Whether they were laid off by downsizing Fortune 500 companies or left their jobs by choice, the number of contingent workers has grown threefold over the past decade to the point where they now make up one-third of the workforce.[15] They are now outside the corporation as part-timers, consultants or other types of freelancers, working out of their home or taking office space as temporary contract workers within company walls. Business analysts have welcomed this transition as a sign that the nation is becoming more adaptive and competitive in relation to changing market forces. We find this analysis shortsighted. A better conclusion is that one-third of the workforce is on the fast track to out-of-date skills and correspondingly low wages. The continuous education that takes place in the average knowledge worker's job is much greater than is generally appreciated. Among the educational benefits provided the full-time worker that often go unnoticed are: formal and informal meetings where knowledge is shared and leveled upwards; implementations of new technical systems, often based on new software and hardware, that teach and reinforce new skills; in-service training and teaching that improves knowledge and skills; and tuition reimbursement or assistance programs that permit full-time workers to enhance their careers through professionally focused education.

By contrast, however much free time contingent workers may have to pursue education, the circumstances of most contingent workers provide neither the incentives nor the opportunities to keep pace with their fully employed counterparts. Without the educational advantages of the workplace, these workers soon fall behind in skill acquisition and generalizable knowledge. It is in the national interest to ensure that all workers, contingent or full-time permanent, be up-to-date in their skills. When fully employed workers enter the contingent workforce, the federal government should provide the workers incentives to continue their education which will better enable them to sharpen and redeploy their skills so they may succeed in their next career. Contingent workers represent a

FIGURE 3.3
Continuity in the Labor Force

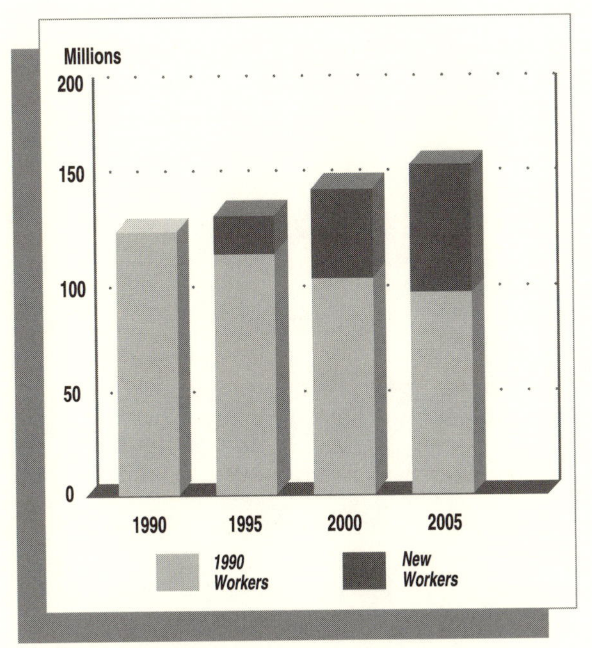

Source: University of Phoenix, Department of Institutional Research Based on U.S. Department of Labor, Bureau of Labor Statistics Data

national asset only to the extent that they are well educated and possess current skills needed by employers.

The Workforce of Today is the Workforce of Tomorrow: Implications for the American Economy

Of the 130 million members of the workforce, 85 percent will still be working ten years from now and, at that time, they will constitute 75 percent of the workforce. Figure 3.3 shows the overwhelming importance of the continuing members of the workforce in comparison to the new workers at any point in time. This conclusion is reinforced by another characteristic of the workforce; it is a mature workforce and it is the more mature workers, at all levels, who exercise the greatest control

FIGURE 3.4
Age Distribution of the Labor Force

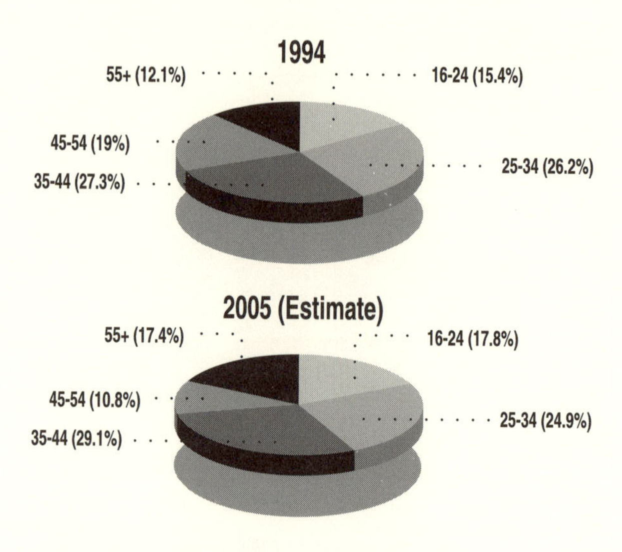

Source: University of Phoenix, Department of Institutional Research Based on U.S. Department of Labor, Bureau of Labor Statistics Data

over the work that gets done. They can be either the most effective agents for change or the greatest obstacles to change. Educating and reeducating mature workers is probably the most effective way to promote the changes that will lead to increased productivity. Especially in need of educational renewal in order to avoid being downgraded is that 10 percent of the workforce that each year changes jobs or occupations.

Figure 3.4 shows the age distribution of the workforce in 1994 and the projected age distribution in 2005. Young workers from ages sixteen to twenty-four represented only 15.4 percent of the workforce in 1994 and only 17.8 percent in 2005. In 1994, the core of the workforce, 73 percent, were the mature workers from ages twenty-five to fifty-four. In 2005 the twenty-five to fifty-four year olds will represent 64.8 percent of the workers but increased life-spans and rising retirement ages will redefine the "mature" workforce at 70 to 75 percent.

Notes

1. In the academic community, diversity usually refers to gender or to ethnic/racial differences. Here, diversity refers to differences in the age and educational purpose regardless of gender, ethnicity or race.
2. The categories were defined using 1994 data. The traditional approach to collecting education statistics makes allocation of the nation's 14.1 million 1992 student population into these six logical categories an exercise in approximation.

   The population data presented here are estimates based on combinations of known population statistics and projections based on known ratios (e.g., undergraduate/graduate and part-time/full-time). Categories 5 and 6 will contain an undetermined number of displaced homemakers and older first-time entrants into the workforce as well as those who are retired or unable to work and who seek undergraduate or graduate degrees. As data become available, the creation of categories 7 and 8 for these two groups would be appropriate. The fact that the definitions and proportions of groups 1 through 6 had to be constructed because they do not exist in any of higher education's databases is further evidence of a lack of focus on the changing needs of an economically diverse student population.
3. American Council on Education, *Research Briefs*, vol. 5, no. 1, 1994.
4. Of the 30,000 working adult students currently enrolled in the University of Phoenix, 61 percent are degree completion students, with a median age of thirty-four years. This percentage has been relatively stable for twenty years.
5. In many fields of scientific and technical study, computer simulations and interactive video have freed instruction from the constraints of the laboratory. The lower costs of electronically mediated instruction will enable adult-centered universities to compete in technical fields and to provide access to these fields to groups previously unable to pursue these studies.
6. One of the explanations for the low graduation rate of blacks and Hispanics, and one favored by Thomas Sowell, an economist at the Hoover Institute, is the fierce competition by elite schools for academically qualified blacks and Hispanics, which leads less-able students in these groups into schools beyond their abilities. Combined SAT scores of 1200 are required for admission to most elite colleges and universities, and the pool of blacks and Hispanics who score that high is very small. For example, in 1992, only 1 percent (n=1,493) of blacks scored 600 or higher on the SAT verbal and 2 percent (n=3,404) 600 or higher on the math. For whites, it was 8 percent (n=55,224) who scored 600 or higher on the verbal and 19 percent (n=132,846) who scored 600 or higher on the math. Because of the small pool of qualified blacks, the elite schools, in their drive for diversity of the student body, admit marginal students who drop out; schools on the next lower rung of the ladder admit the students who couldn't get into the elite schools, but they are again marginal, and so on down the ladder. As a result, thousands of minority students, who would do well if they were well matched with the school they enter, end up dropping out rather than obtaining the degree which they could have earned at a less demanding school.
7. These rates reflect unweighted averages based on unaudited, self-reported data from state institutions for first-time, full-time graduation rates for state cohorts ranging from 1983 to 1985. New Mexico's unusually low six-year graduation rate of nine percent for blacks was excluded from the calculation of average black graduation rates. Because graduation rates are heavily politicized statis-

tics and because the institution's mission must be taken into account in defining and interpreting graduation rates, there is little standardization of the bases for calculation. Some of the difficulty surrounding the acquisition of valid graduation rates will be eliminated as the provisions of the *Student Right to Know Act* are adopted. However, there will still be important differences in educational mission and design which will necessitate great care when comparing statistics across institutions.

8. Audited statistics for six-year baccalaureate graduation rates by race and ethnicity for all students nationwide are not available. These data are based on a 1993 sample of six large, historically black colleges; other colleges declined to respond or could not provide graduation statistics.
9. In eighteen years the University of Phoenix has graduated thousands of minority students and has received only two complaints of discrimination by minority students; one was a foreign national who could not tolerate the interpersonal dynamics of study groups.
10. There is little current data on what percent of employers offer tuition assistance. In 1985, the American Society for Training and Development found that 97 percent of employers responding to a national survey offered tuition reimbursement and the average rate of participation was 5.6 percent. *(Employee Educational Assistance: Who Pays, Who Benefits,* A Report on a Survey of 319 Employers Conducted by the American Society for Training and Development, May 1985.)
11. Based on responses from 858 medium-to-large employers who reimburse tuition. For additional details, see "On Employee Benefits," Hewitt Associates, November 1993, Lincolnshire, IL.
12. Because of recruiting abuses in the trade and technical schools, the U.S. Department of Education (USDOE) no longer permits a university to reward enrollment counselors based on the number of students they enroll. This is but one of many examples of the ill-conceived "reforms" contained in the Higher Education Act of 1992. Without incentives, recruiting efficiency drops dramatically. As a result, hundreds of thousands of working adults whose higher education would benefit themselves, their current and future employers, and the nation will never avail themselves of the opportunity.
13. For discussions of the New Compact, the New Deal, the New Commitment, or the New Covenant, see Brian O'Reilly, "The New Deal: What Companies and Employees Owe One Another," *Fortune*, June 13, 1994; and Robert Waterman, Judith Waterman, and Betsy Collard, "Toward a Career-Resilient Workforce," *Harvard Business Review*, July-August 1994.
14. Not only do most of the managerial and professional workers fail to avail themselves of the educational opportunities offered by their employers, the participation rate among production and service workers is even lower. This is particularly unfortunate because, in some parts of the country, there is a shortage of skilled workers for jobs paying "good wages." For example, in May 1994, Motorola sought to fill 4,000 entry-level positions at a new manufacturing plant in Libertyville, IL. According to an account in the *Washington Post* (May 15, 1994, Section H, p. 1. col. III) "Losing a Numbers Game?", from a field of 40,000 applicants, they were only able to hire 3,000. With 1,000 $10–15 per hour jobs unfilled, Motorola will soon need another 3,000 workers at a new plant in Harvard, IL. Intel faces a similar problem when it seeks to staff large new wafer facilities in Albuquerque and Phoenix.

These labor market conditions would seem to indicate that, at all educational levels, there is a dearth of institutions capable of enrolling, educating, and training workers in the knowledge and skills required by an information-driven economy. (See "Putting U.S. Manufacturers to the Test," *Washington Post National Weekly Edition,* May 30–June 5, 1994.)

15. See Jaclyn Fierman, "The Contingency Work Force," *Fortune,* January 24, 1994.

4

The Economic and Academic Advantages of an Adult-Centered University

If traditional colleges and universities are too costly to operate and are unable to provide either the access or the education needed by working adults, what kind of institution can provide the needed access and education at a price society can afford to pay? Our answer is the *adult-centered university,* especially if it enjoys the accountability and efficiency of being organized as a for-profit entity.

The Economic Advantages of Making Adult-Centered Universities For-Profit Entities

Although adult-centered universities can be either nonprofit or for-profit, based on our experience for-profit universities possess several advantages over the nonprofits we have studied. We recognize that some of these advantages of for-profit status are not due to their *legal* status as a for-profit institution, but to the institutional and individual economic *incentives* that actually define the organization's behavior. The advantages of for-profit universities include:

- They withdraw less federal and state income taxes and local property and sales taxes, and they return more to the public treasury than their students take out in the form of grants and below-market federally insured loans.
- They have access to private capital for funds needed for start-up and/or expansion.
- They operate from leased commercial office space that can be designed to meet student needs and built in a matter of months. This is in contrast to traditional institutions that require years to build costly facilities, many of

which are unused by the majority of students and which may become under-used due to urban population shifts.

- Being responsive to market demands, they tend to expand and grow and are prime creators of "good jobs"—primarily for knowledge workers who require high levels of education, e.g., university faculty and staff.[1]
- They have a highly focused product which is easily inspected and accounted, unlike traditional not-for-profit institutions which aggregate a series of products including learning, lodging, recreation, and socialization into a single budget and accountability unit.[2]
- They relate well to the other for-profit businesses that employ a large majority of the students.
- Like most for-profit organizations, two of their goals are growth and profit, goals which, in the long run, can only be achieved by staying close to the customer and producing a high-quality service that meets the needs of the customer.
- They are managed as well as governed. For-profit universities are managed to deliver a service at a given level of quality at the least cost. The quality management and faculty governance systems help to ensure that the advertised level of quality is met (see appendix A for a detailed case study of an adult-centered academic quality management system).
- They are able to operate with a faculty of working professionals who teach part-time and bring the immediacy of their real-world experience into the classroom. Such a faculty recognizes that the university must seek constantly for efficiency and product-effectiveness.
- A faculty of working professionals not only accepts but also joins management in making needed changes in organizational structures, operating procedures and technology. In sum, the faculty members are constructive agents of change, as contrasted with faculty at nonprofit institutions where they may be opponents of change and may see themselves in an adversarial relationship with the institution's administration.
- By operating year-round and providing students with all the courses they need to complete their degrees, for-profit universities allow students to complete their education and recover their costs in minimum time, thus lowering the rate of defaults on federally insured loans.

Per-Student Costs to the Taxpayer

Since 1992, we have been conducting detailed economic analyses of competing models for delivering higher education to various constituencies. Most of this attention has been focused on models capable of delivering education to working adults. When we calculate the costs to the taxpayer of various models, the overall findings are what might be expected. Public and private higher education cost taxpayers the most, while, if led and managed well, for-profit higher education either does not cost the taxpayer or, in some cases, returns funds to the taxpayer in the form of corporate taxes paid on profits.

The model presented below is not intended to be a completely exhaustive analysis of taxpayer costs under various institutional models. Our efforts to model all costs have convinced us that it detracts from the core message and does not substantially change the cost relationship among the three institutional models.

Decision Alternatives for the Working Adult Student and Their Consequences to the Taxpayer

While the context of higher education programs is diversifying rapidly, their financial structures will fall into three categories established by law: public, private not-for-profit, and private for-profit. A working adult who elects to become a student may or may not consider corporate status when selecting an institution, but this decision will carry enormous financial impact for the taxpayer.

Prior economic models simply determined taxpayer costs for supporting the three basic institutional types—public, private, and for-profit—and per-student costs were determined by dividing total costs by enrollment. Where they could be identified, costs and revenues associated with research and other nonteaching activities were removed from the model.[3] This approach remains valid in that it produces total taxpayer costs; however, it does not isolate the specific taxpayer costs and revenues associated with each working adult student who chooses either a public, private, or for-profit institution. In response to this concern, the model presented below in table 4.1 compares the decision alternatives of these students, whose choice reflects not only an institutional preference but an economic relationship with the public,[4] in terms of each category of cost or revenue.

As the table shows, the taxpayer will underwrite $8,199 of the annual costs to educate a working adult student attending a private college. If the same student elects to attend a public institution, the average annual taxpayer cost rises to $8,634. If this same student elects to attend a private for-profit institution the taxpayer realizes a $101 *profit.*

Table 4.1
Per-Student Costs to Taxpayer by Type of Institution[5]

	Public	Private, Not-For-Profit	For-Profit Adult-Centered (1993)
FTE Enrollment	3,227,993	947,453	21,277[a]
Taxpayer Costs			
Direct Government Support	$6,823	$4,395	—
Tuition Tax Credit Taken by Employers	$91	$513	$271
Student Loans: Market Subsidy and Default Costs	$128	$279	$335
Tax Credit on Endowment	$34	$499	—
Federal, State and Local Tax Exemptions	$1,558	$2,513	—
Gross Taxpayer Costs	$8,634	$8,199	$606
Taxpayer Credits			
Federal, State and Local Taxes Paid	—	—	$707
Net Cost (Credit) to Taxpayer			
Net Cost to Taxpayer	$8,634	$8,199	($101)
Net Cost to Taxpayer With Youth-Centered/Research Expenses Deleted	$7618	$7,590	($101)

[a]Enrollment for working adults is derived by generalization of ratios from known samples.

The components of this model are as follows:

FTE Enrollment. Institutions, especially those that educate working adults, have a high proportion of part-time and occasional students. Basing the analyses on the *full-time-equivalent* reduces but does not eliminate the inequities in aggregating data from the nation's 3,800 colleges and universities.

Direct Government Support. These data include direct funds provided by federal, state, and, occasionally, local governments. Monies come primarily from funding formulas and grants. For-profit institutions receive little or no taxpayer support of this kind.

Tuition Tax Credit Taken by Employers. Employers' reimbursements of employees' education expenses are treated as a business expense. For those businesses not operating at a loss, these expenses would otherwise become taxable income. The bases for determining forgone revenue from employer tax credits produce only estimates. The most recent estimates in this model have come from our work with the Price Waterhouse firm and from several year's data from the University of Phoenix's enrollment survey.[6]

Student Loan Subsidies. Previous Congressional discussion on eliminating most forms of interest rate subsidies for student loans has not resulted in change to the current policy. At present, most types of student loans are made 3.5–4.0 percent under market. The subsidy for these loans is borne by the taxpayer. Likewise, a small percent of loans made to working adult students go into default and are charged back to the taxpayer.[7] Taxpayer costs of subsidy and default are combined on this line of the table.

Endowments. Not-for-profit institutions, especially private colleges and universities, may accumulate endowments that escape taxation in two ways. Private citizens and corporations that contribute to a college's endowment fund escape taxation on that portion of their income. Once received, colleges and universities may then accumulate and invest these funds with both the principal and earnings escaping taxation. On a proportional basis, taxpayer subvention of endowments is especially large for the elite colleges and universities (see Table 2.1 on page 13). For-profit educational institutions are prohibited from accumulating donations and interests free of taxation.

Income and Property Tax Exemptions. Public and private colleges and universities pay no federal, state, or local taxes on their sizable incomes and pay no taxes on the goods and services that they purchase from vendors. Likewise they pay no taxes on their land and capital assets. For-profit institutions pay all of these taxes.

Federal, State, and Local Taxes Paid. Because of the legal definitions of non-for-profit entities, there is no recognition of "profit" on which taxes can be levied. This is strictly an institutional fact made so by the letter of the law; many not-for-profit institutions recognize large financial gains of the kind that the uninitiated would see as profit. Of course, for-profit institutions pay taxation amounting to 50 percent or more on their profits.

In the words of one college president: public institutions are tax *receiving*, private institutions are tax *avoiding*, and for-profit institutions are tax *paying*. Although public institutions do receive the greatest per-student level of federal, state, and local funding, the implied statement that private institutions thus cost the taxpayer little if anything is naive. Such a view makes it difficult to reconcile the vast difference between taxpayer costs of for-profit and not-for profit institutions and the relatively insignificant difference between the two not-for-profit models. The relationship comes into focus by noting that private institutions receive two-thirds the federal, state, and local tax support going to public institutions and, in addition, escape taxation on large endowment draw-downs.

Other taxpayer costs associated with the two models are also higher for the private institution. These costs include:

- Forgone taxpayer revenue on endowments. Endowments, and the forgone taxation on them, do not exist in for-profit private education.
- Taxpayer costs of subsidizing student loans to the market, and underwriting costs on defaulted loans. Default costs are highest for private institutions, primarily because their tuition is significantly higher and students must borrow more money to complete their education. In contrast, for-profit private educational institutions enjoy some of the lowest default rates in the higher education community, because their students are working adults who as a group are more responsible than younger students. Students attending for-profit institutions also do not need to borrow as much money, because the tuition of the for-profit institution is in the lower half of the tuition distribution for private colleges and universities and students complete their course of study in less time.
- Significant forgone taxpayer revenue. Only for-profit private institutions pay taxes on property, purchases and sales; public and private not-for-profit institutions do not. This forgone taxation amounts to several thousand dollars per student.

In contrast to the other two models, the for-profit private institution, if led and managed well, can achieve a 20–25 percent before-tax profit margin which amounts, in the University of Phoenix example, to annual taxpayer revenue of $101 per student.

Although these are striking figures, the information depicted in table 4.1 actually understates the benefits to taxpayers of for-profit, adult-centered institutions for three reasons. First, the model assumes that working adults will be able to retain their full-time employment status while attending school under each of the three institutional models. In truth many, if not most working adults must interrupt or scale down their careers to attend youth-centered institutions. Such an interruption or diminution of employment costs the taxpayer in terms of reduced taxation.

In addition, since the student attending the for-profit adult-centered institution will achieve a degree significantly sooner, any raises and enhanced employment opportunities associated with this educational attainment will transfer money into the taxation revenue stream at an earlier point than would be the case had the student attended either of the alternative institutional models.

Finally, because of the complicated and indeterminable taxation status of gifts made to institutions of higher education, the tax-avoiding nature of gifts to public and private not-for-profit institutions has not been addressed in the data on table 4.1. Since the overall category of gifts to higher education is larger than that of endowments, the inclusion of these forgone taxation opportunities would widen the gulf between tax benefits derived from for-profit and not-for-profit higher education.

The taxpayer has a great stake in an adult student's decision to return to college. Only the student's choice to attend a for-profit adult-centered university does not increase either the federal or state tax burden, while the fact of his/her decision to attend a traditional university does and will continue to do so at a rate two to three times the growth of the CPI.

Allocating Costs of Youth-Centered Education

Critics may point out that some taxpayer support in the form of federal, state, and local funding goes to facilities and services designed exclusively for youth. Net costs associated with recreation facilities, campus housing, student life employees, and athletic facilities, among others, would fall under this category. According to this reasoning, since working adult students do not use these facilities and services, the economic model associated with their education should not consider these costs. In making this valid microeconomic point the larger problem is actually underscored; namely, the extant model of higher education is wasteful, inefficient, and inappropriate to the education of working adults. On more practical grounds, blacking out the costs of identifiable youth-centered and research expenses—neither of which are directly used by the working adult student—has only a small effect on taxpayer costs for educating working adults. Table 4.1 shows the effect in this change in cost allocation. That the change would be slight is a common sense conclusion since the majority of costs in modern higher education are owed to faculty and administrative salaries. Of course, costs removed from the adult-centered side of the table must be added to the youth-centered side, further raising the taxpayer burden.

Capital Costs and Time to Respond to Need: The California Example

The California Postsecondary Education Commission (CPEC) calculates that the cost of acquiring, developing, constructing, and equipping facilities over the thirty-year life of a campus in 1995 dollars is $1,658 per full-time equivalent (FTE) student. Excluding costs for athletic and physical education facilities drops the figure to $1,577. Neither figure includes the cost of acquiring land for the facilities.

Adding a likely least cost for land raises the per student build-out cost to $1,628.[8] CPEC found that the average lead time for planning new campuses is eight to ten years and construction times average two to five years.[9] Yet much of the time and cost of planning and building a traditional campus as well as the cost of operating it arise from the need to provide facilities and services that are neither used by nor useful to working adult students.

In contrast, the for-profit adult-centered model has a build-out cost of $432 per FTE student calculated over the same thirty-year period,[10] and the build out of adult-centered universities can be accomplished in less than six months. Three months are required for planning and site selection and an additional three months are required for construction (building out leased space). Facilities are placed in leased office space that is attractive and within easy commuting distance for students; the only capital costs are for building out classrooms and labs and for furniture and equipment—computers, audiovisual equipment, and so on.

During the time required to build out the leased space, the institutional support systems needed for an adult-centered model can be quickly put in place. The UOP teaching/learning model is a robust, replicable model developed over the past twenty-five years (see appendix A for a case illustration on this) which encourages rapid decision making and little bureaucracy. The systems needed include adapting or incorporating the new facility into the university's academic and administrative computer network, including Internet access for students, faculty, and staff, the training of support staff and the recruitment and training of faculty.

FIGURE 4.1
Time Required to Build a New University and Annual, Per-Student Capital Costs

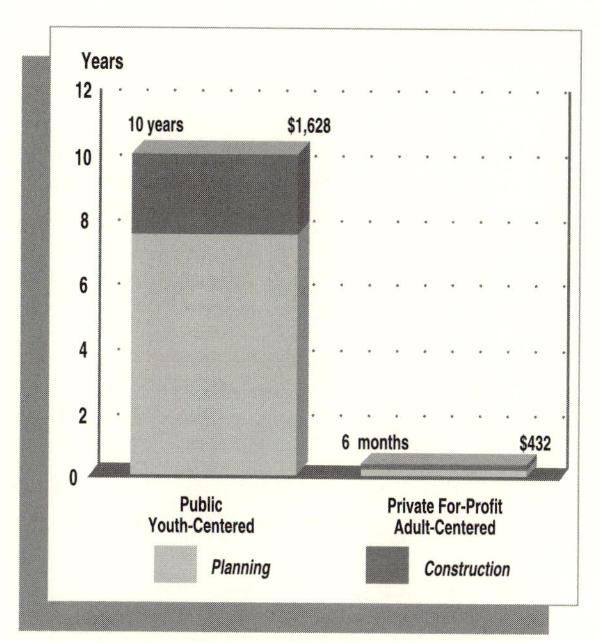

Source: University of Phoenix, Department of Institutional Research and the California Postsecondary Education Commission

In short, an educational facility able to accommodate 500 to 1,500 students can be planned, constructed, staffed, and readied for operation in scarcely more time than the first group of students will require to rearrange their personal and professional lives to accommodate returning to school. The corporate world is appreciative of this kind of responsiveness because it is more in line with their typical time lines.

This same six-month process can be replicated simultaneously in any location where there is a sufficient concentration of students. In areas of insufficient population concentration to support a 500-student facility, distance education is the preferred alternative. Distance education programs can effectively educate working adults via teleconferencing and computer conferencing systems.[11]

FIGURE 4.2
First-Year Costs by Type of Institution 20,000 Student Institutions[a]

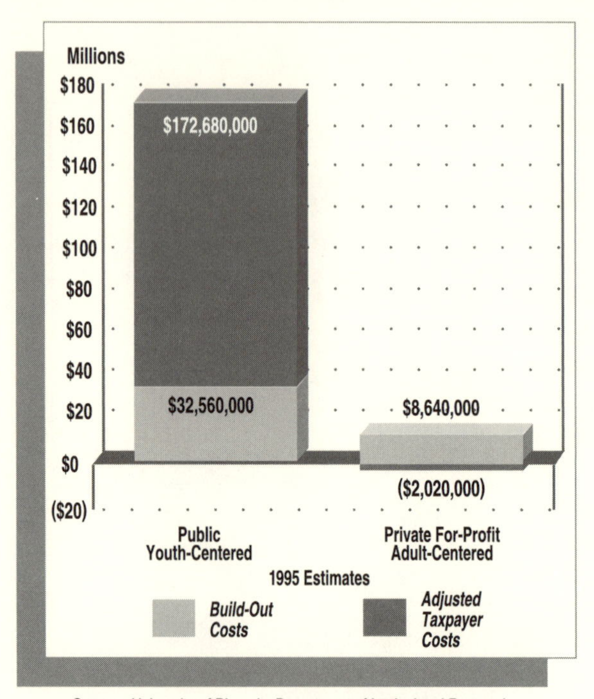

Source: University of Phoenix, Department of Institutional Research
[a] Build-out costs of public institution based on assumption of 30-year bond period.

Except for a two-week break during the Christmas season, for-profit universities function throughout the calendar year on evenings, weekends, and during the day, when they are also used for conferences and training courses. Thus, even before it begins its operations and regardless of who is paying the costs, the for-profit adult-centered university is designed to be more sparing of capital resources, as illustrated in figure 4.1.

Institutional-Level Costs to the Taxpayer

The California example hints at the vast cost differences between the for-profit adult-centered model and extant models of higher education—but it is only a hint in relation to the full picture. Figure 4.2 shows estimated first-year taxpayer costs to plan and build facilities for a university capable of educating 20,000 students under the capital-intensive youth-centered model versus the low capital adult-centered model. As can be seen, in 1995 an investment of at least $172 million was required to place a 20,000 student youth-centered campus in operation for the first year. The same number of students—if attending a for-profit, adult-centered university—would produce taxpayer contributions of approximately $2 million.

The taxpayer savings generated—including the forgone cost of attending a youth-centered institution added to the diminution of tax cost for attendance at the adult-centered institution—would have a direct effect on federal and state support required to sustain traditional systems of higher education. Figure 4.3 is based on cost projections in which two million working adults enroll in either youth-centered or adult-centered institutions.[12] This model projects for the adult-centered alternative a net taxpayer savings of $17.4 billion for the first year. While it is impossible to identify and remove all of the exclusively youth-centered costs of the youth-centered institution (see note 3), the $17.2 billion cost of the youth-centered alternative is based on identifiable taxpayer costs uniquely associated with public and private not-for-profit, youth-centered institutions (research costs and costs directly attributable to youth-only features of these institutions are *not* included in this calculation). These figures do not account for the probable diminished tax revenue when the working adult becomes a part-time worker in order to attend school full time.

Working Adult Students Complete Their Education in Less Time

Figure 4.4 shows that the time required to recover one's educational costs is much longer for students in traditional institutions. In the adult-centered institution, students complete their program of study one course at a time, in a highly structured sequence. The result is that a high percentage of students graduate, most of them on time.[13] It is estimated that the median time to graduation for full-time students exceeds sixty months for youth-centered institutions. At some of these institutions, working adults, most of whom attend part-time, require up to ten years to complete a bachelor's degree.[14]

When combined with the earnings differential, students of adult-centered institutions recover their educational expenditures almost as quickly

FIGURE 4.3
Annual Higher Education Costs for Two Million Working Adults by Type of Institution

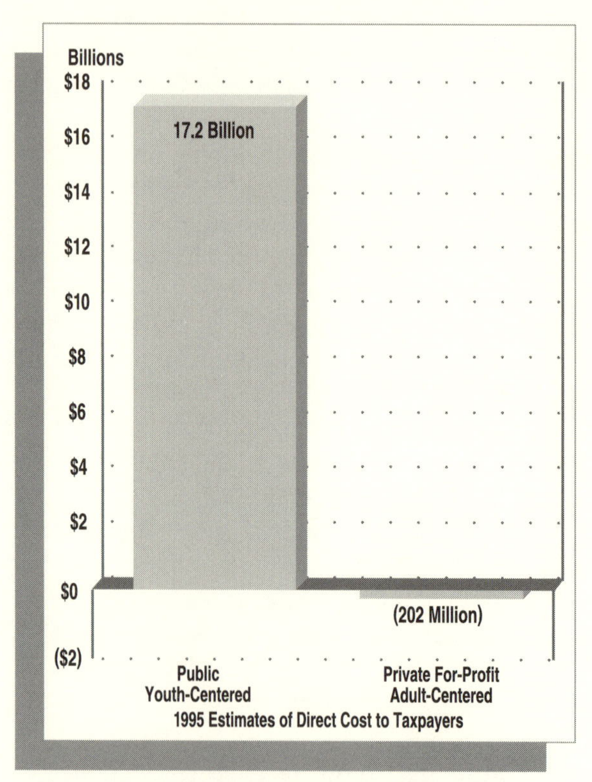

Source: University of Phoenix, Department of Institutional Research

as they incur them. It takes one year for students in an adult-centered university to recover the cost of tuition and fees. Although it takes a similar time for a student at a public university and an adult-centered university to recover the cost of tuition and fees, an adult student who attends a public university must factor into the cost of education the forgone increases in income that would result from earlier graduation from an adult-centered university. Ignoring any forgone income from prolonged attendance, it still takes nearly five years to recover the cost of tuition and fees at a private university.[15]

FIGURE 4.4
Time Required for Working Adult Students to Recover Tuition and Fees

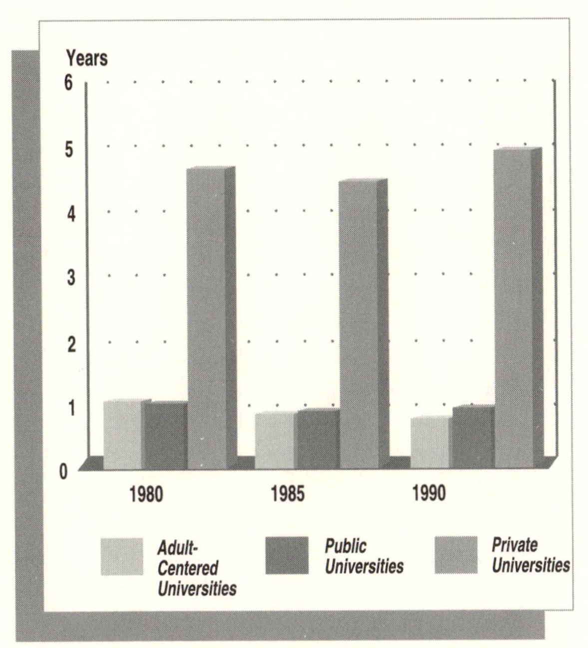

Source: University of Phoenix, Department of Institutional Research Based on U.S. Department of Education, National Center for Education Statistics Data

Summary

Working adults attending for-profit, adult-centered universities place no financial drain on federal, state, or local governments and have education's most enviable record of managing the educational debts they do accrue. Because these students are more likely to place a higher value on good credit, the loan default rate for receiving guaranteed student loans for adult-centered university students is probably under five percent.[16] The least-cost way for the federal government to support higher education for working adults is to provide for the creation of a nationwide system of for-profit, adult-centered universities.

It would be sound economic and social policy to assign to our traditional colleges and universities the education of youth and those seeking advanced degrees in the professions and in academic subjects. This assignment would free these institutions from the responsibility of educating working adults in many job-related fields of study and would greatly reduce the financial pressures that weigh so heavily upon them.

Fortunately, the changes we recommend would not occasion major shifts in how traditional institutions operate. Although hundreds of thousands of working adult students currently enrolled in youth-centered universities would gradually move to an adult-centered university, this would not be traumatic if youth-centered colleges and universities focused on what they do best: educating and training youth and young adults, in all the professions, for entry into the workforce.

Working adults can be educated in a more cost-effective and educationally efficient manner in adult-centered universities. The adult-centered universities, if they are organized as for-profit corporations, can be built with private capital and operated by private firms that, by their nature, will be responsive to the needs of America's businesses, who provide their students. These new adult-centered universities will be unencumbered by the many problems facing institutions that must deal with the socialization of an increasingly diverse student population. Instead of being governed by an academic community divided by discipline into disconnected departments and schools, often at odds professionally and ideologically, these new institutions will be managed with the goal of providing effective education to the working adult educational consumer in a format that meets the consumer's needs. Like any private enterprise, they will be managed for efficiency and profitability.

Unfortunately, as we will discuss in chapter 5, for-profit, adult-centered universities cannot be established in all states. In most states, and all but a few states east of the Mississippi River, state licensure regulations make such institutions difficult to establish, and these regulations effectively bar the entry of any higher education institution that is chartered in another state.

Notes

1. Between January 1, 1990, and January 1, 1996, University of Phoenix enrollments increased from 6,600 to 30,000, and revenues increased from $30 to $120 million. During those years, the University added 697 full-time staff positions, 97 part-time staff positions and 2,060 part-time faculty positions.
2. Robert C. Heterick, Jr. addresses this issue in more detail in the September/October 1995 issue of *Educom Review*.

3. In many cases, this separation is impossible. In our view, the insuperable commingling of the duties of research and publication with those of instruction play a role in the lack of accountability in many institutions of higher education. When asked why there is not more efficient instruction, professors and administrators often invoke the demands of research and publication, and vice versa.
4. Taxpayer costs under the previous models show the same relationship among the three institutional types as shown in the current model. As would be expected, taxpayer costs are generally higher and there is a greater margin between taxpayer costs for public and private institutions and for-profit institutions. One model, for example, produced a $8,600 taxpayer cost for public institutions and a $1,200 revenue for the for-profit model.
5. While the exact costs reflected in table 4.1 will vary with the bases of several key assumptions, the overall relationship of the three sets of costs—public, private and for-profit adult-centered—is relatively constant.
6. The current model assumes that 15 percent of working adult students (approximately 40 percent of the student population) receive employer subvention amounting to 80 percent of their tuition costs.
7. With a current default rate of 3.5–4.5 percent, working adults attending regionally accredited, degree granting institutions have the best loan fulfillment rate of any segment of the higher education community.
8. *Higher Education at the Crossroads: Planning for the Twenty-First Century* and associated technical background papers. All figures are estimates based on source material in the technical papers and were converted to 1995 dollars. In a personal communication (September 1995), Commission staff stated that land acquisition costs have varied from $25,000 to $500,000 per acre for the California State System and that campuses are generally well in excess of 200 acres.
9. Our research shows that California costs and times for planning and construction are comparable with the costs and times required in other states. Only land values vary significantly from state to state and this category of expense represents less than 10 percent of the cost. Some outreach facilities or learning centers can be planned in less time.
10. Unlike calculating costs to the taxpayer, where there is a more firm organizing construct, the fundamentally different financial assumptions of the landlocked traditional institutions and the flexible leased space for-profit, adult-centered universities make comparisons of build-out certain to elicit questions from all sides of the issue. The variations in assumptions are not infinite, however, and the for-profit adult-centered approach will generally be well under $500 per student by any equitable financial yardstick.
11. At the University of Phoenix, students in areas of insufficient population concentration to support a 500-student facility are served by the University's Online Campus and the Center for Distance Education, which provides audiographic and e-mail/fax-assisted courses. Today, these distance education programs serve 3,000 students.
12. This is a projection. At this time, existing for-profit, adult-centered institutions can enroll no more than a few percent of this population.
13. This observation is borne out by University of Phoenix retention and graduation rates, which are above the national average while their length of time to graduation is below the national average.
14. One of the proposed solutions to the lengthening time to graduation is to change course delivery structure and sequence to reduce the time required for a tradi-

5

Critique of Regulatory Constraints

The historical development of private and public institutions of higher education in the U.S. has produced a fragmented market in higher education comprising some 3,500 small, medium, and large public and private colleges and universities functioning in overlapping local, state, and national markets. These 3,500 institutions operate under the rules of over sixty-five accrediting associations, fifty state licensing agencies, the U.S. Department of Education (USDOE), and the U.S. Department of Defense and the Veterans Administration.

Viewed from a broad perspective, regulation—whether by accrediting associations, state agencies or the federal government—is based upon the presumption that it is nearly impossible to otherwise determine the value (educational effectiveness) of a service the consumer has paid for in time and money. Ignoring the clear evidence that the science of educational evaluation is up to the task, the regulators persist in believing that educational outputs cannot be measured. They also believe that consumers of educational services—even intelligent, well-educated adults—cannot adequately judge the value of the services they receive.

Because of these unfounded beliefs, the regulators have constructed a thicket of capital- and labor-intensive "input" standards that they assert will lead to, cause, or are, at the least, necessary conditions to ensure academic quality in the institutions they license or accredit. These input standards include such matters as specifications on physical plant, faculty qualifications, and seat-time-per-credit formulas. They also address the ethical probity of those who operate the enterprise. For many regulators, one of the most important indicators of ethical probity is a non-profit status.

At a time in American history when literally every other sector of the economy has been or soon will be transformed by both domestic and international market forces, higher education remains resistant to innovation and change and diminishes itself in the public eye by responding with suspicion to mounting evidence of a need for change and innovation. One of the reasons innovation and change are viewed as suspect is that most changes will endanger the traditional prerogatives of the faculty and call into question the capital-intensive input standards and operationally inefficient structures that provide and protect those prerogatives.

Systems of education that require less capital and offer more efficiency are generally viewed as serious threats to the status and authority of tenured professors and administrators. This extensive regulation by federal and state agencies and by the federally authorized private accrediting associations reinforces the reluctance of colleges and universities to change in response to the rapidly changing needs of the society and the economy.

Part I: Accreditation

Accreditation and the Quest for "Quality"

The accrediting bodies whose powers are most far-reaching are the six regional associations that grant general accreditation to the colleges and universities in their region and have the ability to undermine almost any educational innovation. As figure 5.1 shows, the regional accrediting bodies are: the Western Association of Schools and Colleges, Middle States Association of Colleges and Schools, Northwest Association of Schools and Colleges, North Central Association of Colleges and Schools, Southern Association of Colleges and Schools, and the New England Association of Schools and Colleges.

During over nearly a century of operation, the regional associations have made major contributions to the maintenance of diversity and quality in American higher education and have been instrumental in the creation of a system that many academics and politicians are proud to declare "the finest system of higher education in the world." Unfortunately, in their efforts to maintain this "finest" system, the regionals often work to inhibit change.

There are several reasons for this reluctance to encourage change, but surely the most important is the power of the faculty to resist change and place its interests before those of the students and the public. One of the

FIGURE 5.1
Regional Accrediting Associations

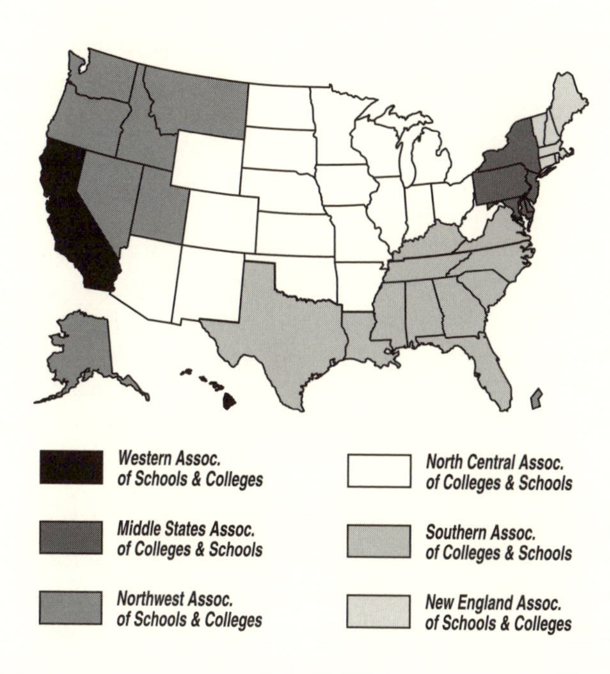

basic principles of accreditation is protection of faculty control of the educational process. This entails the protection of faculty prerogatives which includes the faculty's right to resist change. On balance, the academics who run the accrediting apparatus believe that only an institution governed by a full-time faculty can be considered an "institution of higher education." Faculty power resides in control of academic production and product—what the students are taught and what the students "learn." The core of this production function is general education and as the North Central Association Handbook of Accreditation states, "faculty have ownership and control over general education."

The political right charges the radical professorate with corruption of the youth and failure to address the needs of society. These are charges that began in ancient Athens and will be repeated when our own civilization is considered ancient. The critics on the right believe that the solution to the reform of higher education is to change the professorate. Nothing could be farther from a solution. If they got rid of the "radical" faculty members, their "conservative" replacements would no less eagerly corrupt the youth or be any more willing to address society's needs than their radical predecessors. When they function as a group, almost all members of the professorate are institutional conservatives and, whether left, right, or center, they are protective of their prerogatives and will resist any change that threatens those institutionalized prerogatives. Every society needs conservative institutions for stability and traditional colleges and universities are one of our most important conservative institutions. Ultimately, it is a question of balance. At what point and for what reason does an institution cease to preserve the past and serve the needs of the foreseeable future? At what point and for what reason does the higher education community recognize that institutions dedicated to the preservation of our culture must also be balanced by institutions dedicated to securing an uncertain future?

The reluctance of accrediting associations to initiate change in existing institutions or encourage the formation of new institutions stems in part from the attacks against them from politicians of both parties and the public intellectuals of the right. An example of one of these attacks occurred during the drafting of the Higher Education Act of 1992. During the debates on the bill, the regional associations were charged with failure to prevent the student loan default problem, a charge that was far from the truth. Whatever their failures might be, failing to prevent high student default rates is not one of them. Regionally accredited four-year colleges and universities have minor default problems. Only the public community colleges that are regionally accredited had serious default problems and those problems arose from the characteristics of the student population rather than any dereliction on the part of the regionals.

Most of these attacks are, in our opinion, unjustified and arise from misunderstanding what accrediting associations are all about. Critics want the association to police institutions and impose standards that will guarantee exemplary graduates. Putting aside the fact that no system of policing higher education could accomplish this result—exemplary graduates are largely the product of exemplary freshman—the accrediting associations have performed very well the functions they were designed to perform. Accrediting associations are based on the principle that once an institution has demonstrated that it possesses and maintains the basic characteristics of an institution of higher education, it should not be policed; rather it should be aided and encouraged to improve itself. This process is accomplished by institutional self-study and emulation of the best practices in peer institutions. For all its faults, accreditation has protected an open system of higher education from the proliferation of substandard institutions—there are no regionally accredited diploma mills—and, on the positive side, it has been a vital part of creating the American system of higher education which, for all its faults, is still considered to be one of the "best in the world."

The Congress, especially the staffs of the education committees, did not let these facts blunt the attack on the regionals. In order to prevent future, highly improbable, default problems among colleges and universities, the regionals and all the institutions they accredit are now subjected to much more rigorous oversight because the regionals have been mandated to enforce a large number of very prescriptive rules and regulations promulgated by the USDOE. While the impact of these rule changes has been modestly effective in cleaning up the default problem in the public community colleges, they have further strengthened the resolve of most institutions to avoid change.

The best solution to satisfying new educational needs, the instant case being higher education for working adults, is to create new institutions to perform this function. The accrediting associations could play a positive role in this process if they would free themselves from the belief that the basic characteristics of legitimate institutions of higher education must all be those present in traditional colleges and universities. To free themselves from their traditional paradigm, they would have to begin with what the final product of the new institution is to be—that is, what knowledge and skills will such an institution provide for its working adult students that would enable them to improve their performance on the job and what knowledge and skills their employers are willing to pay for them to obtain. Once this is established, they could then determine what inputs and processes would be needed to produce the final product. Certainly, it would not be the set of inputs found in traditional institutions; rather it would be a new set, some traditional and some new. We are of the opinion that it would be a set much like the one for the adult-centered institution we have described. Unfortunately, the regional associations now do as much to inhibit needed change as they do to promote it.

Substantive Change: The Catch-22 of Accreditation

Of all of the accreditation rules that impede innovation, the most damaging are those dealing with substantive change. These rules make meaningful innovation time consuming, tedious, and costly and almost ensure that a college or university will not be able to respond to rapidly changing economic and social conditions. Substantive change is the catch-22 of accreditation: Any institution that wants to meet the changing needs of society through innovation appears to be showing symptoms of instability and should be required to demonstrate its stability by staying the same. Institutions that stay the same are urged to change, but are rewarded for their stability. "Substantive change" rules of the regional associations anchor our institutions of higher education comfortably in the past.

All of the regional associations are publicly committed to change and innovation, but their rules often belie their "philosophical" statements. For example, the Western Association of Schools and Colleges defines a "substantive change" by an institution as that "which may significantly affect its quality, objectives, scope, or control" thereby covering almost any change an institution might contemplate. Under such rules, a quick response to changing market conditions is impossible; before undertaking a substantive change, an institution must submit a report to the Commission *"at least 120 days in advance of the proposed change"* (italics ours). Upon reading the report, the Commission may require an on-site visit by an accreditation team before approving or rejecting the change. The Commission cautions, "In the event Commission action is required, no assurance can be made that the substantive change review process can be completed by the time of the next Commission meeting. Institutional actions are taken by the Commission only at its June and February meetings." Even if a private institution of limited resources makes what it believes to be an adequate investment in facilities and staff, there is no assurance that the Commission will find it adequate, and the school can very well end up losing its investment. If an institution tries to speed up the process by implementing a change before it has been approved by the Commission, it can be placed on "probation" and ultimately have its accreditation taken away.

The other accrediting agencies have similar barriers to substantive change. The Southern Association of Colleges and Schools requires that "before any significant changes are made in purpose, programs, scope, location, ownership, level of operation, or instructional delivery systems, the institution must notify the Executive Director of the Commission on Colleges in writing *"at least one year in advance of the proposed change"* (italics ours). In its "Code of Good Practice in Accreditation," the New England Association vows "to encourage sound educational experimentation and permit innovations"; the Association then proceeds to list the usual items that trigger the substantive change regulation.

Until 1993 the North Central Association made an explicit commitment to the support of an institution's need to change in response to changing conditions. It was this commitment that enabled the University of Phoenix to gain accreditation and then to grow and prosper:

> The Commission [on Institutions of Higher Education] recognizes that change within the institutions affiliated with it is as constant and rapid as it is challenging and inevitable.... Consequently, it does not attempt to interfere with an institution's efforts to respond creatively to the many internal and external forces which demand that it develop and modify its functions and operations if it is to grow or, often, even survive.

However, after being pummeled by Congress in hearings on the Higher Education Act of 1992, the 1993 Handbook of Accreditation greatly attenuated this commitment:

> The Commission is supportive of educational innovation and change necessary to improve educational quality. However, the Commission has a responsibility to seek assurance that institutional changes...are both appropriate to the institution and within the institution's capability of providing with quality.

This statement inhibits an institution's attempts to change. No matter how well documented an institution's capability to effect a change might be, before it can even begin the process, it must prepare a comprehensive plan that first goes to North Central's staff for review[1] and, no matter how often an institution has demonstrated the ability to successfully carry out a similar change, the staff review is followed by an on-site visit for any change that adds a degree level, introduces a new program, opens a new site either in the U.S. or abroad, or delivers a program through some distance education medium. After suggested revisions in the plan are made by the site visitors, the request goes to the Commission for final approval. All of this takes nine months to a year, and only then can an institution safely commit the resources needed to effect the change. By then the change might well be no longer worth the time and expense.

The substantive change rules of all of the regional associations go a long way in explaining why colleges and universities are so slow to respond to the needs of business and industry and have lost so much of the business education market to training companies. When businesses have a need for educating their employees, their planning time frames are in weeks or months, while those of higher education are in years.

Part II: State Regulation

State Regulation of Higher Education Market

Based on twenty-five years of experience dealing with licensing agencies in twenty-three states, we are confident in asserting that state regulation does more to restrain trade in higher education than either the accrediting associations or the federal government. Higher education is one market where the original constitutional devolution to the states has led to regulatory excess and restraint of trade. This area requires major reform. The laws and regulations governing private higher education in a majority of states are designed to limit competition and bar the entry of out-of-state institutions. In all but a few states, the administrative and academic standards of traditional, capital-intensive institutions are the basis of licensing requirements regardless of whether their mission is to educate youthful full-time students or adults who work full-time and attend classes evenings and weekends. Traditional institutions require a full-time faculty, usually tenured with Ph.D.s, library buildings, labs, dorms, student unions, and athletic facilities, none of which is required by working adults. Regionally accredited adult-centered institutions, even if they are licensed in a dozen states where they have demonstrated their effectiveness, are often denied licensure for "lack of quality" because they have an untenured practitioner faculty, many without Ph.D.s, an electronic library and computer labs, but no dorms, student unions or athletic facilities.

Rather than allowing the market to determine need for an institution's programs, thirteen states require applicant institutions to "demonstrate" the need for their programs and eight of these states either require approval from local competing institutions or they give local institutions an opportunity to meet the "demonstrated" need before licensure will be granted. Illinois divides the state into geographical areas and gives exclusive rights to local institutions and New York gives exclusive rights to certain degree programs to institutions...all this in the name of efficiency. In state-funded schools, it may make sense to divide programs across schools. For institutions that do not use state funds, however, this makes little sense. Ten states do not recognize the adequacy of a practitioner faculty or an electronic library with full-text searching, immediate document delivery and inter-library loans for hard-to-find books; instead, they demand a full-time faculty and a building with books. Two states, Oklahoma and Pennsylvania, bar all for-profit institutions of higher education. Most states have loosely worded regulations and give a wide latitude to the decision-making body that administers them. As a consequence, it is almost impossible to challenge a negative decision. Appendix C sets forth the basic regulations for the fifty states in a table with keys indicating the type of regulatory restriction.

Barriers to entry range from the obvious to the subtle. States such as New York are blatant; they simply state that they want no competition to local institutions and reject all applications from out-of-state colleges or universities seeking licensure. States with more subtle regulations profess fairness and objectivity but then use procedural barriers to entry. Usually, these states allow or require comment and/or approval by the local institutions that would have to compete with the out-of-state institution. In Illinois, an applicant out-of-state institution must host, at its own expense, a meeting of representatives of all institutions that believe they might be affected if a license were granted. The meeting ends with a vote of those assembled on whether or not to recommend the application. At the meeting to consider the University of Phoenix application, thirty-nine institutions attended and the vote was 39 to 0 not to recommend. In North Carolina, the State University Regents make the decision and, if any local institution offers or is willing to offer the same programs as the applicant institution, then the application is denied. In Minnesota, an application is first reviewed for recommendation by a committee representing local institutions—the University of Minnesota, the State Community College System, and the State Association of Private Colleges and Universities. And, in Michigan, an applicant institution must be approved by a Committee of Scholars, drawn from local institutions, who visit the home campus of the applicant institution before making its decision. In sum, our experience indicates that most state higher education agencies operate as trade associations that are mainly concerned with policing markets; they have little involvement in, or need to be involved in, consumer protection.

The activities of state regulatory agencies are strongly influenced by the State Higher Education Executive Officers (SHEEO). We have observed that the network of SHEEO members ensures that regulations instituted in one state will be looked upon favorably in other states. At its annual meeting in 1989, SHEEO viewed with increasing concern:

> ...the growing practice by nonprofit institutions [private colleges and universities] of establishing far-flung branch and "storefront campuses" and courses through telecommunications. Those developments have created an environment in which students can no longer rely on an institution's accreditation as an assurance of quality at all its locations.[2]

Indeed, many of these "far-flung" activities serve the adult market, and they are staffed with part-time instructors and have a limited investment in fixed capital and facilities. Some of these programs *are* of questionable value. This is particularly the case when a struggling private college operates off-campus programs as cash cows, with any profits flowing back to support the institution's campus-based programs. Whatever the "quality" of these programs might be, however, they are usually of the same quality as the adult programs found at the home campus. SHEEO would be better advised to look at all of the adult programs of such an institution rather than restricting its concern to the "far-flung" branch campuses.

*The Diploma Mill Shibboleth**

Although it might seem odd to the lay person, one of the arguments state regulators use to justify such regulation, particularly of "off-campus" programs, is to protect consumers from "diploma mills." The Washington, D.C. higher education establishment, the staffs of most state higher education agencies and their state legislative allies have, over the years, claimed that diploma mills and the bogus degrees they sell constitute a major danger to educational consumers and the public at large. Further, they claim that most of these diploma mills are the result of the failure of state governments to regulate adult education programs. The few diploma mills that exist are all outside the system of regional accreditation.

---

* See Appendix B for more discussion on the issue of diploma mills.

Regularly, one finds news reports decrying the existence of diploma mills and the need to toughen regulations. The state most often cited is California, whose diploma mill problems lie in licensing laws that permit the licensing of unaccredited "institutions of higher education."[3] No matter how carefully drawn, such statutes permit diploma mills disguised as legitimate institutions to obtain a license. The remedy is not more regulations but less. All a state needs to do is to license only degree-granting institutions that are regionally accredited or can demonstrate that they are making reasonable progress toward accreditation. *No state with such a statute has any diploma mills.*

Who can recall a press report of a public servant or prominent individual who having been exposed as claiming a bogus degree, had claimed one from a diploma mill? Who would claim a bogus degree from anything less than a reputable institution? SHEEO estimates that 30 million Americans have gained employment using fraudulent credentials. If there *are* 30 million Americans who have gained employment without a legitimate degree, rather than conjuring up 30 million degrees from diploma mills, the more reasonable explanation is that 30 million people have doctored their resumes by claiming a bogus degree from a reputable university (usually a large state university with hundreds of thousands of graduates).[4] They can get away with it because they know that employers do such a poor job of checking references.[5] While it is in the national interest to eliminate diploma mills, the excessive and oppressive regulation created ostensibly to deal with this small problem has had large deleterious effects on educational innovation.

Restraint of Trade in Higher Education

Statistical data on institutional restraint of interstate trade in education by the states are not readily available but can be assembled. The most conclusive evidence for restraint of trade is data on the number of institutions of higher education operating outside the state in which they are incorporated and what percentage they represent of the total market for higher education within each state. These data are not gathered by the federal government or any of the state governments. The data for this book were assembled by first surveying the higher education agencies of the fifty states in order to obtain a list of the out-of-state institutions licensed to operate, or known to be operating, in each state. The second step was to inquire of each of the named institutions whether they were operating in the state and how many students they enrolled. Not all of the institutions were forthcoming with the information, but it was almost always possible to obtain the enrollment figures from a cooperative member of the staff. All but one of the institutions were private, since almost all public institutions only operate out-of-state at federal installations, primarily on military bases. Because of the disparate sources for the data, it was not possible to reduce reported enrollments to full-time equivalents.

These data were first gathered in 1988 and again in 1993. In 1988, of the some 3,500 private colleges and universities, approximately 115 had out-of-state operations and ten operated in more than two states. The estimated enrollment in out-of-state programs was 36,000 students, which represented 1.5 percent of total private higher education enrollment. By 1993, increasing regulatory restrictions by state agencies and accrediting associations had reduced the number of institutions operating out-of-state from 115 to 34. Only nine of these institutions operated in more than two states. Out-of-state programs had a combined estimated enrollment of 47,000, which again represented 1.5 percent of total private higher education enrollment.[6]

Figure 5.2 offers graphic evidence of the effects of restraint of trade in higher education. In twenty-eight states there are no students enrolled in programs operated by out-of-state regionally accredited institutions; eight states have less than two percent; and nine have two to five percent. In eleven states, including the industrial states of New Jersey, Connecticut, Pennsylvania, and New York, no out-of-state institution can be licensed to operate. The fact that only 1.5 percent (estimated) of private higher education enrollments are in institutions operating out-of-state is evidence of the extent of the restraint of trade in educational services. As the map shows, western states place few or no barriers on out-of-state institutions and, except for Georgia, from the plains states to the Atlantic, the barriers range from substantial to total.[7] These data also show the error of claims by the officials of colleges, universities, state agencies and accrediting associations that there is a "proliferation" of out-of-state programs that endangers educational "quality."

By restraining trade in educational services, local institutions can monopolize the educational market free from the presence of competing educational products and services and thus face fewer pressures to innovate or improve either their productivity or the quality of their services.

FIGURE 5.2
Percentage of Higher Education Enrollment in Out-of-State Institutions

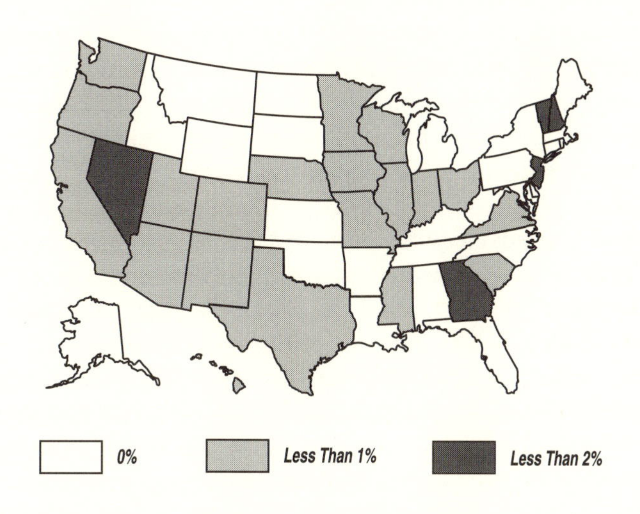

Source: University of Phoenix, Department of Institutional Research

Part III: Federal Regulation

Introduction

Other than the G.I. Bill, the first major post-World War II entry of the federal government into the financing of higher education came in the Higher Education Act of 1965. This act created the student financial aid programs that slowly grew to $11 billion annually by the 1990s; as the volume of loans grew, so did the default on those loans. The rising level of defaults prompted Congressional action that came in the form of the Higher Education Act of 1992. Prior to 1992, the federal government had done little to change the regulatory structure of higher education as set forth in the Higher Education Act of 1965. This structure was based on what was called the Triad—(1) the states licensed all varieties of postsecondary institutions, (2) the accrediting commissions accredited them, and, once they were accredited, (3) the federal government provided much of the money to run them.

The Higher Education Act of 1992 altered the power relationships of the Triad. In addition to being the source of the money, the federal government assumed the power to enforce the regulations that affect the use of the money. The 1992 act placed the power of enforcement in the hands of the USDOE, which was authorized to mandate standards and procedures for both the accrediting associations and the state higher education agencies. In the view of Congress, neither the accrediting associations nor the state licensing agencies had been sufficiently vigilant or effective in regulating the institutions they accredited and licensed. The attitude of those who drafted the 1992 legislation was exemplified by David V. Evans, staff director of the Senate Subcommittee on Higher Education, who stated, "We basically believe that what we should be doing is putting institutions through as many hoops as possible."[8] The result has been heavy and prescriptive regulation that created yet another barrier to the changes that higher education needs to make if it is to play a significant role in economic renewal.

The conceptual framework of the 1992 act was carried over from the rules and regulations of the accrediting associations and state agencies. Higher education was conceived as being youth-centered and campus-based and the student population was assumed to be homogeneous with regard to age and work status.[9] The statute and the rules and regulations flowing from the statue were written to fit that conception. Not only did Congress prescribe, it attempted to "democratize" postsecondary education by practically eliminating the term "postsecondary" from the legislation and replacing it with "higher education," the term it applied to all institutions from dog grooming schools to Ivy League universities.

Impact on the Accrediting Associations

Instead of collegial associations devoted to the improvement of member institutions, the regional accrediting associations have been mandated as enforcers of federal regulations, among which include requirements to establish:

- controls that guarantee that the association consistently applies effective mechanisms for evaluating compliance with its standards;

- program standards that address the full range of an institution's offerings, including those portions conducted at branch campuses and off-campus locations;
- input standards that address: curricula, faculty, grading, facilities, equipment and supplies, financial and administrative capability, student support services, recruiting and admissions practices, academic calendars, catalogs, publications and advertising, graduation rates, employment prospects, program length and tuition and fees in relation to subjects taught, including quantitative cost factors that, if exceeded, trigger special review and adverse action;
- output standards that measure student achievement by grades, theses/portfolios, standardized tests, completion rates, job placement rates, employer evaluations, alumni follow-up studies, and other recognized measures of educational outcomes;
- methods to analyze and evaluate the documentation furnished by an institution, and any appropriate information from other sources, to determine the compliance with agency standards of the entire institution;
- oversight and monitoring of institutions between accreditation and re-accreditation visits, including conducting unannounced visits when noncompliance is indicated;
- a comprehensive and detailed policy on evaluating any substantive change in an institution's operations; before a change can go into effect, the institution must notify and receive prior approval of the change; and
- a mechanism for prior approval of any change that is off-campus, for which an institution must prepare a business plan covering revenues, expenditures and cash flow, the physical resources and the management. After approval of the plan, the accrediting body must conduct an on-site visit as soon as possible but no later than six months from program commencement; only then can the change be presented to the accrediting commission for final approval.

Conclusion

Congress should eliminate the fiction that there is something called "higher education" that includes everything from auto mechanics to quantum mechanics and pass legislation that reflects a more accurate view of the differences among postsecondary institutions and the populations they serve. Certainly, if Congress expects to see more of the kind of higher education that will play an effective role in economic renewal, it should distinguish between trade schools and institutions of higher education and between youth-centered, campus-based institutions and adult-centered, community-based institutions.

State licensure and federally mandated regulations combine to make it difficult to create the system of adult-centered universities needed immediately by working adults. Chapter 6 concludes this book with a recommendation for legislation to create such institutions that would allow adult-centered universities that serve the educational needs of the American workforce to operate interstate. State regulation of higher education needs reform and federal statutes need some revision. Both can be accomplished by legislation that creates nationally authorized adult-centered universities.

Notes

1. With only seven staff members to oversee nearly a thousand institutions, timely staff review by the North Central Association is problematic at best.
2. See *The Chronicle of Higher Education*, September 9, 1989.
3. "California Trying to Close Worthless Diploma Schools," *New York Times*, August 31, 1994.
4. A College board member discovered that the man who, after years of service at the College, had been promoted to President, claimed a degree from the University of Arizona that he didn't have. A reporter, checking the Board member's credentials, discovered that she, too, was claiming to have a degree from the University of Arizona that she had not earned. Both the President and the Board member were forced to resign. Had the Board member kept her mouth shut, both she and the President would probably be in office today.

   Then there were the events leading to the appearance of a bumper sticker in Phoenix in the winter of 1986 which read, "I Flew With the Duke." Its inspiration was the fall of Duke Tully, the publisher of the Arizona Republic, Arizona's premier newspaper. Tully was a man of towering ego and arrogance who wielded enormous power in the state. Unfortunately for him, he had concocted a resume that not only claimed a degree in electrical engineering from Purdue, where he dropped out after one year, but also a distinguished military career as a fighter pilot in Korea and Vietnam. "Lt. Colonel" Tully even served as honorary vice president of the Arizona Air Force Association before he was unmasked, to the delight of most of the people of Arizona.
5. Robert Half, the international search firm, conducted a survey in the U. S. and Great Britain to determine opinion on the accuracy of resumes. The survey found that most American managers are willing to accept the resumes of job applicants as being accurate; not so the British. Thirty percent of British personnel mangers don't believe the resumes are accurate and the group as a whole believe that 70 percent of job candidates "either lie or are economical with the truth." (See "Many lies in work records," *Daily Telegraph*, September 7, 1990).
6. There is no uniformity, state by state, in counting the number of students enrolled in private institutions. Sometimes students in out-of-state institutions are included in state totals; sometimes they are not. The data presented are based on our best estimates. Even though these estimates might be slightly under- or overstated, any discrepancies would have only a slight effect on the percentages.

In 1993, the University of Phoenix and DeVry, Inc., were the two largest of the thirty-four institutions operating out-of-state. UOP then enrolled over 15,000 of its 20,000 students in seven states outside of Arizona. This figure represented 32 percent of out-of-state enrollments for all institutions, nationwide. DeVry, Inc. had an out-of-state enrollment of some 15,000 traditional-aged students in technical and business programs in seven states. DeVry also operates the Keller Graduate School of Management that enrolled 650 out-of-state adult students in MBA programs in three of the states where there are DeVry campuses. DeVry and the University of Phoenix accounted for over 64 percent of the national out-of-state enrollment.

7. The University of Phoenix was recently granted permission to establish campuses in Florida, Lousiana and Michigan. At this time, only Michigan has begun to serve significant numbers of students.
8. See *The Chronicle of Higher Education*, September 9, 1989.
9. The regulations were prejudiced against for-profit institutions and the Secretary was allowed great discretion to amplify that prejudice. See Appendix D for a discussion of the different treatment accorded for-profit and not-for-profit institutions.

6

Federal Action to Create a National Market in Higher Education Services

The best way to introduce effective competition, innovation, and continuous improvement into the higher education market is for Congress to place higher education in the stream of commerce by mandating uniformity in state licensing standards and procedures or by providing for nationally authorized institutions of higher education.

States' Control Over Higher Education vs. Technological Change

Given the long tradition of the states' Tenth Amendment-based claim to control over education, there is no way to avoid state resistance to any federal action that would preempt state laws regulating higher education. Under the banner of consumer protection, states have, especially during recent years, expanded the extent and "rigor" of their regulatory activities in their attempts to exclude "bad" institutions and promote "good" institutions. However, because state regulation is primarily designed to protect institutions rather than consumers, it does more to deny access to "good" education than it does to protect consumers from the "bad."

No matter how ardently state regulating entities argue the sanctity of the Tenth Amendment, there is sound precedent for preemptive federal regulation of activities that at one time were the province of the states, for example, railroads, airlines, electric power, securities exchange, telephone communication, radio, television and, now, banking. In each instance, technological change created a national market that made state regulation irrational, anticompetitive and ineffective. As communications technology increases in its scope and effectiveness, the U.S. economy is being knit ever more closely together, and companies that operate nationwide are almost pleading for federal regulation to free them from state regulations that add needlessly to the cost of doing business.

Even some of the professions are seeking relief. For example, lawyers are questioning the interstate barriers to legal practice arising from the "crazy-quilt" of state bar admission rules. The solution to this problem is the creation of a national bar. The fact that such a move is spearheaded by the American Corporate Counsel Association gives it some chance of success since large corporations will support a national bar as a way to lower legal costs. In the business environment, according to the Association, "Uniform laws are increasingly appropriate because, as a nation, we're far more [economically] homogeneous than we ever were a generation ago and certainly 200 years ago."[1]

Changing communications technology is also creating a national/global market for the production and sale of electronically delivered higher education, and programs are being delivered across state lines by a variety of colleges and universities. This blurring of state lines arises in part from the fact that over 60 million people live in urban areas that cross state lines. Another reason institutions are operating outside the state in which they are chartered is the emergence of a new kind of educational institution—the for-profit, adult-centered university. In addition to the desire of these institutions to exploit the profit potential of new markets, for-profit universities usually have invested their capital in standardized programs and computer information systems that are only financially viable if their costs can be spread over a large student population. The only thing that keeps for-profit universities from entering all states with large urban markets is state constructed barriers to entry.

Distance Education: A Regulatory Window of Opportunity

Fortunately, the development of ever more effective electronic modes of delivering education from a distance has challenged the tradition of unfettered state control over education. This new movement presents an opportunity for the federal government to rationalize the higher education market by making it possible for colleges and universities to operate interstate without having to meet fifty different licensing requirements and six sets of regional accreditation criteria. Today, American institutions can offer electronically delivered education over the Internet to students living in every nation that has a telephone system. Neither the fifty states nor any nation can control this activity. A 1995 InterEd survey found that 40 percent of the nation's institutions of higher education already offer one or more forms of technologically mediated distance learning,[2] a number approximately 10 percent higher than CCA and Associates found in a 1994 survey.[3] InterEd's projections are that growth will persist until the year 2000, when fewer than 10 percent of the nation's colleges and universities will be without one or more forms of technologically-mediated distance learning. Institutions in England and the countries of Western Europe are already offering their distance education programs to an international audience. If the federal government does not place higher education in the stream of commerce, free from irrational state control, it will be impossible for American institutions to develop the critical mass and the expertise to participate in and gain a significant share of the global higher education market.

State licensing and accreditation officials have been almost immune to the larger forces affecting the delivery of higher education in these new modalities. They continue to view higher education as a local or state delimited activity and they believe that the historical interpretation of the Tenth Amendment giving states the control over education is a sound basis for their constitutional right to continue the Balkanization of the higher education market. They accomplish this by using regulation to exclude "outside" institutions from their states. They thereby protect local institutions from competition by those "outside" institutions whether these "outside" institutions offer campus-based or distance education.

State control over the licensing of distance higher education, delivered by one or more electronic modalities, has elicited some of the most trenchant discussion of the whole complex of issues involved in the regulation of higher education. Between 1982 and 1984, the Project on Assessing Long Distance Learning via Telecommunications (Project ALLTEL) addressed the problem of state regulation of distance higher education from a national perspective. ALLTEL was sponsored by the State Higher Education Executive Officers Association (SHEEO) and a now defunct organization, the Council on Postsecondary Accreditation (COPA) that represented the seventy-plus accrediting associations recognized by the USDOE.[4] The organizations that sponsored ALLTEL sought to deal with the incommensurability of fifty different state licensing regulations and six different sets of regional accreditation criteria for institutions that offered distance education via electronic means.

ALLTEL's central recommendation was to place primary responsibility for ensuring the "integrity and quality" of an institution's distance education programs on the home state's licensing agency and the appropriate accrediting association, whether regional, national, or specialized.

This recommendation requires the institution to prepare a "profile" designed by Project ALLTEL that, when certified by the home state, would be given to the authorities in other states where the institution sought to offer its distance education programs.[5] However, providing the profile would not trigger reciprocity since the other states could request additional information and conduct visits to any receiving site within the state before granting a license to operate. There was no concerted effort to implement use of the "profile."[6]

In 1991, the New York Regents hosted a meeting of thirteen states and Puerto Rico on state regulation of distance education. The main recommendation repeated that of Project ALLTEL: an institution's home state and regional accrediting association would have primary responsibility for licensure and accreditation. There would then be a signed agreement among the states granting reciprocity. However, as of this writing there has been no more willingness to grant reciprocity than there was in 1985. No state has signed the agreement to grant reciprocity and there is no reason to believe that any of them will.

The emerging view among state education officials is that states need to regulate institutions that offer distance education programs because it is "often difficult, if not impossible, for a regional accrediting group to ensure the quality of courses delivered thousands of miles away from its region."[7] Given the ease of air travel and the sophistication of telecommunications—phone, fax, teleconference, video conference, and computer conference—we consider the citing of geographic limitations to the quality of accreditation to be disingenuous. This is especially so in light of the fact that thousands of corporations are quite effective in administering global operations. Electronic communication is instantaneous and air travel is hardly arduous.

The "naiveté" among academics with regard to oversight at a distance is a measure of their refusal to recognize that technology will inevitably change higher education forever. And it is indefensible to argue, as too many state officials do, that the consumers of higher education must be protected from themselves because they are unable to distinguish inferior from superior education: "States do have a legitimate interest, and an obligation, to see that their citizens are not educationally defrauded, or tricked into accepting inferior education when a superior variety is readily available."[8] So long as students choose regionally accredited two- or four-year colleges or universities, there is little danger of consumer fraud. When students choose something other than a regionally accredited institution, and it turns out to be inferior, it is almost always a case of a knowing and willing buyer and seller.

Deregulating Regional Accreditation

In order to free commerce in higher education services, it is also necessary to remove the anticompetitive barriers erected by the regional accrediting associations. Although most of the regionals permit an institution to operate in any state where the institution has a license, entering a new state constitutes a substantive change, requires an elaborate plan and triggers an accreditation visit. The whole process usually requires a year or more; once permission has been granted, the regulations add needless costs to any operation at a distance.

Currently, under pressure from the USDOE, the regionals are in the process of negotiating common standards for all of the regions; it would not be a radical step for them to negotiate standards for institutions with authority to operate in all fifty states.

Alternative Methods of Protecting Interstate Commerce in Higher Education

There are several ways to accomplish federal protection of interstate commerce in private higher education. Obviously, publicly supported institutions are the province of the public entity that funds them and would not be eligible for designation as nationally authorized institutions. However, Congress could declare that private higher education is in the stream of commerce and is therefore exempt from restrictive state regulation. Or, Congress could pass legislation that enforces reciprocity among state licensing agencies—a private college or university chartered in one state could then apply for licensure in the other states. Or, the USDOE could require uniform state licensing of private higher education and reciprocity as a requirement for institutions to participate in federally funded programs for higher education. Although each state would still grant a license to operate an institution of higher education, it would be more difficult for a state to deny a license to an institution already licensed in another state. None of these solutions are likely to find acceptance in Congress and only a declaration by Congress would actually place higher education in the stream of commerce.

As a small step in what will undoubtedly be a long journey toward the achievement of a national market in private higher education services, the Phoenix Institute has drafted proposed legislation that might be acceptable to Congress and that would create a national market in private higher education services while maintaining state licensure and regional accreditation. In order to minimize the opposition of traditional institutions and state licensing officials, we have chosen to limit the sphere of federal action to private institutions that seek authorization to operate interstate, and, in order to have consistent accreditation standards, these institutions would agree to be evaluated by standards that are primarily outcome driven rather than input driven. Such evaluations are expensive and cost eight to ten times as much as traditional institutions, on average, spend on outcome evaluation of any kind. However, well-documented outcome evaluation is the only way any regulatory entity can monitor institutions operating multiple campuses nationwide. As we have discussed, input standards invariably force institutions into capital intensive facilities, full-time faculties, and mandated hours of seat time per credit, and none of these are relevant to an adult-centered institution.

Institutions eligible for national authorization would be those which have a mission to provide education to members of the workforce and which have embraced learning outcome assessment as the basis upon which the institution is to be evaluated by the appropriate state licensing agency and accrediting association and remain under the continuing oversight of the USDOE. Traditional campus-based private institutions wishing to restrict their operations to the state in which they are chartered would remain under current state regulations.

Concepts for Federal Legislation—Findings

In the Higher Education Act of 1986, Congress established adult postsecondary education as necessary to promote a competitive workforce. The 1986 Act found that:

- It is in the interest of the federal government to support continuing education for adults in order to reduce unemployment and underemployment; to enhance job opportunities; and to promote a well-trained, flexible, internationally competitive workforce and an educated citizenry.

- The increasing incidence of relocation and dislocation of industries and workers, their entry and reentry into the workforce, and the rapid rate of change in technology, the economy, population demographics, and social conditions necessitate significant improvement in the opportunities for higher education for adults in all stages of life.
- The majority of working adults who continue their education do so for job- and career-related reasons.
- Access to postsecondary educational opportunities is limited for adults whose educational needs have been inadequately served, or whose economic or personal circumstances...are barriers to such opportunities.
- The organizational structure and administration of postsecondary institutions often represents a significant barrier to matriculation for the adult learner and such institutions need to adapt themselves to integrate adult learners.
- The federal government should encourage the development of institutional partnerships between the public and private sectors and postsecondary institutions for the purpose of planning and implementing effective educational programs and services for the adult learner.

Additional Findings Indicated by Present Conditions

We believe that if Congress were to revisit the subject of adult higher education, it would find that most of the 1986 findings are still valid and, in addition, it would find the following:

- Members of the workforce currently lack adequate access to higher education that addresses their need for education that is time efficient, convenient and professionally relevant.
- The accessibility, effectiveness and efficiency of distance education would make higher education available to those individuals for whom other systems of postsecondary education do not or cannot adequately serve.
- There are now over 6 million working adults enrolled in America's colleges and universities, and there are millions more who would enroll if there were adult-centered universities that offered programs suitable to their needs.
- The regulatory structures required by many states and accrediting associations present barriers to the expansion of institutions that could meet the needs of these working adults.
- It is in the interest of the federal government to protect interstate commerce in higher education so that adult-centered universities capable of meeting the needs of working adults can be free of conflicting state regulation and the irrational constraints imposed by accrediting associations.

Recommendations for Congressional Action

In order for universities seeking to operate interstate to make a significant contribution to workforce quality, it will be necessary for the U.S. Congress to enact legislation that:

- provides such institutions authorization to operate nationwide, free from unreasonable restrictions that might be imposed by the various states;
- designates these institutions of higher education as "nationally authorized universities";
- recognizes that nationally authorized universities are distinct from private colleges and universities that operate within the confines of one state;
- establishes the defining educational and administrative characteristics of nationally authorized universities; and
- establishes the requirements whereby the U.S. secretary of education would grant the status of "Nationally Authorized University."

Characteristics of Proposed Legislation to Grant Authority for an Institution of Higher Education to Operate Interstate as a "Nationally Authorized University" and to Provide for Federal Regulation Thereof

Definition of a Nationally Authorized University

Such a university is:

1. Organized as a corporation;
2. Has as its primary mission the education of adults, especially members of the workforce, by means and methods that are appropriate to their professional and personal requirements (a member of the workforce is defined as a person who has a minimum of three years experience working in a chosen trade or profession);
3. Has a license to operate as a degree granting institution of higher education from the state in which it is incorporated and is recognized as an accredited institution of higher education by a regional accrediting association;
4. Has a faculty composed of working professionals with appropriate academic credentials beyond the bachelor's level and with a minimum of five years of employment as successful practitioners in their profession and who are no more than twelve months removed from practice in the subjects they teach;

5. Offers instruction at times and places that are convenient to students' work and/or home;
6. Is organized and managed so as to treat the students as the primary consumers of its services and seeks constantly to meet their needs as articulated by them;
7. Is organized and managed so as to treat the employers of its students as secondary consumers of its educational services by being responsive to the educational needs of its students as articulated by their employers;
8. Provides to the secretary current enrollment and financial data in a format to be specified by the secretary;
9. Provides to the secretary, on a schedule to be established by the secretary, data obtained from continuous, statistically valid information:
   a. from the consumers of its services about the quality and timeliness of all components of its services, including instruction, curriculum, text materials, support services, facilities and administrative services;
   b. about its teaching-learning system including the educational inputs and processes (e.g., curriculum, instruction, and student services) and the learning outcomes (e.g., the knowledge, skills, attitudes and values) that are needed and used in the student's workplace;
   c. on how it uses the results of all of its quality management measures to improve the quality of its educational programs and the degree to which those programs meet the needs of the primary and secondary consumers; and
10. Meets required standards of portability across employers through adherence to defining characteristics 7, 8, and 9 and the establishment of cooperative relationships with employers.

Proposed Authority of the Regional Accrediting Associations

Accreditation of nationally authorized universities should be conducted by the apposite regional accrediting association using standards that are consistent with the terms of the statute creating such institutions. Each regional association will recognize the accreditation of institutions holding national authorization. The secretary shall withdraw recognition from a regional association that has not established standards for nationally authorized universities and/or does not recognize the accreditation by another regional accrediting association of a nationally authorized university.

Proposal for a Certificate of Authority to Provide Higher Education for Working Adults

Upon receipt of evidence that an institution of higher education, meeting the definition of a nationally authorized university, possesses a state license as a degree granting institution of higher education and is accredited by a regional accrediting association, the secretary would give to the university a certificate evidencing that such institution has complied with all of the requirements in connection with the provision of higher education for adults, especially members of the workforce, and that such institution would be authorized to provide the same anywhere in the United States, the District of Columbia, Guam, Puerto Rico, and the U.S. Virgin Islands.

Proposal for Preemption of State Law

An institution holding a certificate of authority under the proposed legislation, and that has been issued a license to operate as an institution of higher education by the state in which it is organized and that has been accredited by an accrediting association approved by the secretary, shall be deemed in compliance with all relevant laws and regulations required by the legislation. The provisions of such legislation would supersede any and all state laws insofar as they may relate to the provision of higher education for members of the workforce.

Renewal of Certification

Certification must be renewed every five years. Renewal requires the following:

- The institution's state license and accreditation are current and the institution is in good standing with the relevant state agency and regional accrediting association;
- A self-study submitted to the secretary evidencing the institution's adherence to the mission of a nationally authorized university is examined and approved; and
- The institution's operations, as described in the self-study, are reviewed by a panel appointed by the secretary. The panel will recommend renewal, deferral with corrective action or denial of continued status as a nationally authorized university.

Notes

1. See "Firms Ask Congress to Pass Uniform Rules," and "In-House Lawyers Fight Interstate Barriers to Their Legal Practice," *Wall Street Journal*, May 10, 1993 and November 26, 1994.
2. InterEd, Inc., a Phoenix firm, conducted a fax-back survey of chief academic officers at 1,250 accredited colleges and universities over a 30-day period during the summer of 1995. Recipients were asked to indicate if they provided technologically assisted distance education and, if so, what kind of delivery system(s) they employed. Those offering technically assisted education at a distance were asked to indicate whether the education was offered on a for-credit, degree and/or continuing education basis.
3. *Understanding Information Systems in Higher Education: Report to Respondents,* 1994, CCA Research, Wellesley, Massachusetts.
4. COPA endeavored to speak for the accreditation community and to make some national sense out of the disparate policies and actions of its many members. COPA was killed when the six regional associations, who provided most of the money and most of COPA's prestige, decided that COPA was more of a liability than an asset and resigned from the organization.
5. Chaloux, B.N., "The Project on Assessing Long Distance Learning Via Telecommunications (Project ALLTEL): A Summary Report," *The Council on Postsecondary Accreditation* and the *State Higher Education Executive Officers Association*, 1985.
6. For a discussion of Project ALLTEL and subsequent attempts to achieve reciprocity in state licensing of institutions of higher education see Kevin P. Reilly and Kate M. Gulliver, "Interstate Authorization of Distance Higher Education via Telecommunications: The Developing National Consensus in Policy and Practice," *The American Journal of Distance Education*, Vol. 6, No. 2, pp. 3–16, 1992.
7. Kevin P. Reilly and Kate M. Gulliver, "Interstate Authorization of Distance Higher Education via Telecommunications: The Developing National Consensus in Policy and Practice," *The American Journal of Distance Education*, Vol. 6, No. 2, pp. 3–16, 1992.
8. Loc. cit.

Epilogue

Higher Education and the "Jobs Crisis"

The jobs crisis was building for years before it erupted in the 1996 Republican presidential primaries. Labor Secretary Robert Reich had given countless speeches on the subject but it was the passionate rhetoric of Patrick Buchanan that brought the issue to political life. The jobs crisis certainly throws a spotlight on the arguments put forth in the preceding chapters. Why, one can reasonably ask, should a person devote the time, money and energy needed to earn a bachelor's or master's degree when tens of thousands of degree holders have been downsized, riffed, laid off, let go, or fired and are now flooding the mails and the Internet with their resumes. The only positive note in this scenario is that, bad as the situation is for a degree holder, it is worse for someone without a degree. The accelerating bifurcation of the wage structure into those who have the necessary education and those who do not sends a clear message: securing appropriate postsecondary education combined with worklife-long education is the best way to insure the economic stability of individuals and families.

The jobs crisis also raises the more general question of whether or not advanced education for all members of the workforce who are intellectually capable is good public policy. Is advanced education necessary for most of the jobs that will exist in the coming decade? If not, will the aspirations of millions of degree holders who are overqualified for their jobs pressure employers to upgrade jobs and introduce ever more sophisticated products and, perhaps, make America ever more the dominant economy of the twenty-first century? Or, will those millions of degree holders be condemned to spend a working life-time in jobs for which they are over qualified? The experience of less developed countries provides cautionary evidence that large numbers of unemployed degree holders does not always push employers to upgrade either products or jobs. Mexico has a surplus of engineers, architects, accountants, doctors, dentists, and lawyers and tens of thousands of them are engaged in menial labor, often as illegals in the U.S.

Already, the U.S. has the highest percentage of degree holders among industrialized countries and the highest unemployment rate among degree holders. Large numbers of college-educated unemployed with high expectations is not healthy for any society and can be dangerous. Such a population is susceptible to demagoguery and to arguments that the state should provide jobs directly or force private employers to provide the needed jobs. Even though unemployed college educated workers might represent a political danger, one must still ask whether, in the long run, a country will prosper in the global economy without a college educated world class workforce? In the long run we're all dead but this doesn't mean we should avoid planning for the long run. Whatever our present discontents, it seems evident that a nation's success in a global economy requires massive investments in human capital, especially in the form of higher education—it is the only way to maintain a world-class workforce.

We believe the preceding chapters argue persuasively that the least cost way to a world-class workforce is through for-profit higher education, that is, if world class is defined as a workforce with 25 percent or more college-educated workers. And, for the individual, still the best way to secure a middle-class income is to obtain a college education. The current economic issues of stagnant incomes for the lower 90 percent of the population, massive downsizings and escalating executive salaries, bonuses and stock options, and rising economic insecurity has now called into question the value of higher education both for the nation and for the individual.

Worker Animus Toward Corporate America

Unfortunately, the world-class workforce that created and produced the technology and the organizational structures that have made the U.S. economy the world's most productive, has not shared equitably in the benefits of increased productivity, and the share of those millions of college-educated workers who have been downsized, has been close to zero. The failure of millions of workers to benefit from their increased productivity has led to a growing animus toward corporate America among all levels of the workforce. This animus has raised angry voices and pushed the issue of job security, wage stagnation and economic inequality to the top of the political agenda; it seems certain that public sentiment will require some government response, the question is what?

How do governments of other industrialized countries address problems that many say are aspects of globalism and seemingly beyond the control of national governments? In Japan, where there is a culture of corporate paternalism, redundant workers are tolerated and layoffs are usually restricted to part-time workers and those who are not considered career employees, especially female clerical workers. Also, executives make a quarter to a half of those in the U.S. and there is much less income inequality. As a result, unemployment is almost nonexistent by U.S. standards, and resentment toward corporate executives and social anxiety are very low. European companies have also resisted the pressure to downsize. Europe has strong unions, executives that make far less than their U.S. counterparts and with a compensation system that will not make them rich by using downsizing to drive up the value of their stock options. Strong unions and more socially oriented management, coupled with a strong safety net for those who are laid off, greatly lowers economic anxiety. In the long run, either economically or politically, an economy cannot sustain millions of redundant and unemployed workers but, as yet, there is no endemic economic security in either Japan or Western Europe.

In contrast with Japan and Europe, American political and economic elites, both Democrat and Republican, believe that a free-market economy must accept the pain of creative destruction. It is accepted as the price of progress and the source of better days in the future. Most members of these elites do not suffer much of the pain themselves but they do respond when the cries of pain among the workers gets so loud it cannot be drowned out by other vocal interest groups. Even though politicians may say "I feel your pain," a free-market ideology greatly circumscribes their possible responses to the problem. The Democrats count the working class as a core constituency but, in a weekly radio address that responded to the jobs crisis, President Clinton offered little more than moral suasion as an anodyne for worker economic anxiety.

> Let me make clear: the most fundamental responsibility for any business is to make a profit, to create jobs and incomes by competing and growing.... We recognize that not every business can afford to do more than worry about the bottom line, especially a lot of small businesses. But may of America's most successful businesses have shown that you can do well by doing right by employees and their families.

He then outlined five ways that "enlightened businesses," in mostly voluntary cooperation with workers and government, should help improve employee's lives: by being "friendly to families" with flexible work schedules and child care; by giving better health and pension benefits; by offering improved education and training; by working "in partnership" with employees to cope with fluctuations in profits and productivity, and by assuring a safe workkplace.[1]

When one lists the identified causes for the economic anxiety—a deflated minimum wage, weak unions, the impact of legal and illegal immigration, rapidly changing technology, the decline of manufacturing and economic globalization—Clinton's remarks make clear, there are no quick-fix remedies available to the free-market ideologue. As a result, most of the remedies being served up by politicians and economists are long term and none of them deal with the immediate reason for declining wages and corporate downsizing—the shift in the balance of power from labor to capital. As Lawrence Mishel of the Economic Policy Institute writes:

> Workers in every industry you look at, including those that are the most technologically advanced, have been losing ground.... If every one is afraid that the job they have is the best they can get, because if they lose it, they go to a worse job, then no one—white collar worker, blue-collar worker, union or non-union—is able to put any pressure on the employer.
>
> It is not a skills deficit that is killing the American worker, it's the wholesale loss of clout. Fearful workers are quietly taking whatever employers dish out.... Productivity improvements, like all other benefits, go automatically to the corporate side of the table, where they are turned into profits. There is no longer any need to spread the wealth. The folks at the top of the pyramid, at least for the time being, have won.[2]

It is depressing to contemplate but, at least for the time being, the balance of power between labor and capital is not going to shift and the problem of economic insecurity in America, if it has a solution, will be long term. And what are the proposed solutions? A $500 per child tax cut, a flat tax, reduced welfare benefits and forced self-reliance, minor immigration reform, a small reduction in corporate subsidies, and decreased government regulation.

All of these remedies are designed to unleash entrepreneurial energies, stimulate economic growth, and lift all boats. Unfortunately, none of them, either singly or collectively, is going to produce a rate of economic growth sufficient to create high wages jobs faster than technology eliminates them. The consensus among economists of all persuasions point to an annual growth rate of 2.2 to 2.5 percent and nothing politicians have proposed is going to raise that figure more than one or two tenths of a percent. "It might be good politics if some candidate acknowledged this," said William Kristol. "If candidates did, and the public accepted the verdict, ...then a new set of policies and campaign promises would almost certainly have to arise. *They would focus not on how to make the economy swell, lifting all boats, but how to live with the modest growth that is possible.*"[3] Given the reality of slow growth, candor seems to require us to recognize that the market alone is not going to change the balance of power between capital and labor sufficiently to bring a semblance of equality. Until there is a more equal balance, the jobs crisis and endemic economic insecurity are not going to disappear.

The only way the balance is likely to change is though some form of government intervention, for example, a higher minimum wage, a law barring striker replacements and tax breaks for companies that actually train and educate their workers. Such remedies are anathema to free-market ideologues but the growing animus toward corporate America will eventually make such remedies more and more politically palatable. In the meantime the nation needs to train and educate its workforce even if corporations offer little incentive to workers being trained and educated. Ironically, the desire for economic survival will supply the incentive.

Fortunately, along with God and motherhood, both Democrats and Republicans support training and education, but there is little agreement on who will do the training and education and who will fund it. There is little possibility that Congress will appropriate the money to fund the number of workers who need either training or higher education. Corporations could, and would, provide much of the high skills training if they were provided adequate incentives but they cannot provide the needed higher education. While offering the mandatory praises for American business, even the president of the National Association of Manufacturers, Jerry Jasinowski, recognizes that business is not delivering the needed education and training: "the average company spends roughly 1.5 percent of its payroll on employee training and education. To my mind, that figure needs to double." He then called for "employment security":

> The United States still offers the best employment opportunities in the world. But if it is to stay that way, it will require a new social compact in the workplace. That doesn't mean guaranteed job security—which is impossible in today's highly competitive world. But it does mean guaranteed employment security; ensuring that

> workers acquire the training and skills to move up the ladder, if not at one company, then at another.
>
> For employees, it means instead of thinking of themselves as victims, they should be investing in their own futures. And, in exchange for their hard work, they should insist that corporations keep up their end by helping to fund the cost of training, and by rewarding financially those who help themselves.

For-profit higher education can provide the needed workforce higher education the nonprofit and public institutions cannot. Only institutions that deliver bona fide higher education, with measured effectiveness, to students who are full-time workers can provide the needed services and bona fide means education delivered in a useful format at the times, places, and prices required by working adults. The few traditional institutions that provide such services do not have the needed capacity and expanding that capacity is simply too expensive for the tax payers to fund and, and to expensive for the students to attend.

The $1,600 per student capital cost of buildings and equipment and the $7,500 it costs the taxpayer for each student each year makes the cost of expanding the present system prohibitive. Only for-profit institutions can be expanded to meet the demand without a burden on the taxpayers. Furthermore, working students cannot afford a traditional college education. Even if the present system—full-time faculty teaching full-time students—could be expanded to meet the educational needs of millions of workers, the workers could not afford to attend. Half the cost of attending a traditional college or university is foregone income and the higher the income, the higher the cost of education. The cost to a person who leaves a $40,000 a year job to attend a two year MBA program is $80,000 plus the $80,000 and up it costs for tuition, books, and living expenses. Not many workers are willing to spend $160,000 for a degree because it is not likely to be a good investment. When foregone income and the expense of supporting a large campus are removed, the cost of a two, three or four year degree drops into the $5 to 15,000-a-year range and becomes a good investment for millions of workers.

Although politicians recognize the need for workforce higher education and bemoan its prohibitive costs, they are so locked into traditional assumptions they cannot recognize the tested solution that lies at hand. Perhaps this analysis and argument will offer them a new vision from which to address the problem of how to educate a world-class workforce and at a price taxpayers are willing to pay. We have shown them a way that is affordable and effective. All they need to do is recognize this new model for higher education and understand that this model cannot grow to a capacity that can meet the nation's higher education needs until it is free of the constraints of state-by-state regulation.

Notes

1. "Clinton, in Ohio, Asks Industry To Share With Their Workers," *New York Times*, March 24, 1996.
2. "A Job Myth Downsized," *New York Times*, March 3, 1996.
3. "Trickle Down: It's a Slow Growth Economy, Stupid," *New York Times*, March 17, 1996 (the author's italics).

Appendix A

The University of Phoenix: A Model for an Adult-Centered Professional University

This appendix sets forth a model for institutions capable of providing the education and training that managers and professionals need. It explains the components of the model—their rationale, how they function, how they are evaluated and what they produce. The model is based on the University of Phoenix; similar institutions could be replicated within one year or less in any urban center in America if the rules of state regulation and regional accreditation made it possible. If such institutions were created throughout the United States, they would contribute a major improvement to the quality of the labor force and the functioning of the American economy.

Education for Working Adults

The practical, worldly philosophy of education that undergirds the University of Phoenix harks back to the nineteenth century when many of today's elite universities were founded. Senator Leland Stanford, the founder of Stanford University, dreamed of a system of education that would make "the humblest laborer's work more valuable," would "increase the demand for skilled labor" and would "wipe out the mere distinctions of wealth and ancestry." Like Stanford's original conception, the University of Phoenix seeks to dignify labor, to increase both the demand and supply of skilled labor, and to create genuine access for the disadvantaged.

Perhaps the most important part of the University of Phoenix model is the fact that it is a robust working model, having successfully educated over 65,000 undergraduate and graduate working adults since its inception in 1976. From its inauspicious beginnings, when the first class enrolled eight students in Phoenix, Arizona, to its present enrollment of over 30,000 students in twenty campuses located in eleven states, Puerto Rico, and throughout the world via its Online and Distance Education campuses, the university has grown to be a major provider of adult-centered higher education. The University's educational model has proved itself to be both robust and adaptive; it has weathered precipitous changes in local and national economic conditions and equally abrupt changes in needs for specific educational services. It continues to adjust, rapidly and efficiently, to the changing needs of the workforce while achieving annual growth rates that lead the education industry.

Education at the University of Phoenix proceeds from explicit academic standards and practices. These standards mirror the productivity, quality, efficiency, innovation, and attention to process required in the best practices of the workplace. Students learn not only from the curriculum and faculty, but also from the infrastructure formed by the principles that guide the selection of faculty, the creation of curriculum and the provision of educational support services.

The following sections set forth the basic components of the university's educational or "teaching/learning" model. By understanding each of these components and their interactions, the synergy of the model can be understood and appraised.

Students: Agents of Change in the Making

Students at the University of Phoenix are today's managers, supervisors, technicians, production specialists, teachers, health care providers, counselors, service personnel, trainers and other agents of change in the workplace. All of these people have two things in common: they have meaningful experience in the adult world of work, and they seek greater skills and a better place in tomorrow's work environment. As such, they come to the classroom prepared to learn and to teach. They also come with a mature understanding of the nature of the work environment. University of Phoenix students play an active role in both governance and in the teaching/learning process. They are required to share their knowledge and expertise with their fellow students and their instructors, to be active participants in their classes and study groups, and to provide feedback to their instructors and to the administration on the quality of the instruction, curriculum, facilities, equipment and administrative services.

Reservoir of Experience. University of Phoenix students understand applied subjects with greater depth, practicality and realism than students who can draw only on abstract ideas to explain what a real-life problem might look like. The ability to make practical connections between what is learned in the classroom and its application in tomorrow's work environment is a powerful force for learning; it increases the pace at which information can be presented and, at the same time, increases the quality of the learning experience—more is learned in less time.

Practical Focus. Students have clear and direct needs to acquire practical skills they can apply immediately to their jobs and professions. In this sense, they actively seek to raze the overworked dichotomy between training and education. They want both, and they want them to occur in the same classroom at the same time.

Student-to-Student Learning. Students teach each other using knowledge gained from personal and professional successes and failures, workplace training they have received and delivered to others, and their observations of the experiences of other employees. This "horizontal" learning can be extremely timely and relevant.

Faculty: Facilitators of Change

At traditional universities, the emphasis on youthful, residential students affects not only the scheduling and location of classes but the teaching style as well. Knowledge is assumed to reside primarily with the professor, whose job it is to transmit it to a largely passive younger generation. While this method may be acceptable to youthful students with little experience in the professional world, it annoys and alienates working adults, who deservedly feel that their extensive experience is being discounted and dismissed.

University of Phoenix faculty teach at night what they do during the day. To be able to effectively integrate theory and practice in the classroom and to assist their students in carrying out ambitious work-related projects, they must possess attitudes and skills quite different from those found in traditional faculties. The University of Phoenix has radically restructured the role of the faculty, whose members function as teachers, consultants, mentors, and facilitators of learning. They do not function as professors of a discipline or as ultimate arbiters on the subject of their expertise. In a class of experienced adults, many students are likely to be as knowledgeable as the faculty member on a particular subject. Consequently, it is foolish for a faculty member to hold him- or herself out as the sole source of knowledge or the ultimate arbiter on all of the subjects discussed in a course.

Faculty Selection, Development, and Evaluation. Developing and maintaining a faculty in the adult-centered tradition is a complex and labor-intensive process that rewards the University and its students and faculty many times over. It is a continuous process of selecting, mentoring, evaluating, and coaching classroom behavior toward a standard of excellence that is satisfying both to the instructor and to his or her students. Experience has shown that successful University of Phoenix instructors share a common set of characteristics: they have theoretical and working knowledge of the subject; they are not dogmatic; they are interested in sharing their knowledge and skills with others; they are not threatened by the possibility of having students in their classes who are more knowledgeable than they are about the subject at hand; they are comfortable working in small groups; and they support the University of Phoenix concept that a faculty member is both a facilitator and a conduit for learning whose main responsibility is to assist students in acquiring the knowledge and skills set forth in the learning outcomes for the course in whatever way is most appropriate for them.

Curriculum: A Repository of Best Practice

Tradition has it that curriculum development is largely in the hands of the individual instructor. Curriculum committees at the university, school and department levels, if they exist, may endorse textbooks and suggest reading lists, but how a subject is taught, what is required of the students and what learning outcomes will be met and evaluated is almost always at the discretion of the individual faculty member. From the viewpoint of quality management, such a system lacks necessary components. There are no specified learning outcomes, the instructional process is limited to the style and skills of each instructor and there is excessive subjectivity in judging the amount and quality of what the students have learned. In such cases, very bright students learn well at the cost of their less academically talented classmates who will learn less than they would have under a more effective learning environment. The University of Phoenix determined that there is a more thorough and consistent way to develop and validate curriculum; following are the key elements of that way.

Ties to the Professional World. Programs and curricula are developed to serve not only the professional needs of the students, but also the needs of the secondary consumers—the companies that employ them.

Structured Best-Practice. In the curriculum development process, a degree program begins with the assembly of a task force of faculty and industry professionals who identify best-practice and determine the objectives of the program and the content to be covered. From the objectives and the content emerge a set of courses constituting the "core curriculum" for that degree program and each student in that degree program must complete this core curriculum.

Specific and Measurable. The curriculum sets out specific learning outcomes for each course; where possible, outcomes are stated in terms of skills, competencies, and other performance-related measures. To support this level of scrutability, curricula embed materials, exercises, and assignments in a body of effective instructional strategies. It is not unusual for faculty members to remark that there were more activities to support the educational process than could be implemented in the duration of the course. This excess is by design. The assumption is that instructors need a range of activities to meet the unique needs of each group of students.

"Trans-curriculum." Common to virtually all of the university's curricula are course outcomes, aimed at developing generalizable skills, competencies, attitudes, and values known to be associated with success in the workplace. Examples of this trans-curriculum include: the ability to think critically and analytically; to work efficiently toward a common goal within a team; to present ideas effectively in written and oral communications; and to cooperate with others who may have conflicting goals.

Continuous Improvement. All courses are field-tested, evaluated, and revised prior to their adoption throughout the university. Once a course is installed, data from the Student End-of-Course Surveys, Faculty End-of-Course Surveys and the Student Comment Analysis System are provided to instructors, curriculum design specialists, and program heads to determine if the course is meeting its design criteria and is doing so comparably at all of the university's campuses. Curriculum is under continuous evaluation and revision to address current issues in the field. On average, courses are completely revised every two years.

Although the faculty are required to deliver a structured curriculum and to do their best to see that the students achieve the specified learning outcomes, the university does not impinge upon their academic freedom. Students and faculty are free to discuss any and all subjects and express any opinion they wish so long as the core learning outcomes are achieved. By providing the curricular materials, training, and constructive feedback on results, both the university administration and the instructor know to what extent students are actually achieving the learning outcomes.

Colleges and universities often view the educational experience as a simple and direct relationship between an instructor and a class of students. Little attention is paid to the structure of the classroom, which is typically a room with a lectern, seats arranged theater style and the instructor either lecturing or conducting a lecture/discussion. Research on these models has consistently found them to be inefficient, but these studies have done little to change an 800-year-old tradition. Since the classroom is an important place in the teaching/learning process, the University of Phoenix model places emphasis on structuring the environment and measuring the effects.

The primary mechanisms for controlling the learning environment rest with faculty selection and training, and with curriculum development and validation, but the instructor's work is made more effective by creating a favorable psychological and physical environment. The first step in achieving the desired environment is to eliminate the irrelevant. Classes are held only once a week at facilities located to reduce commute time to less than fifteen minutes for most students. Where possible, services are delivered to the student. Registration and the payment of fees occurs by phone, by mail, or prior to class in the classroom; texts and other course materials are delivered to the classroom or by UPS to the student's home. Classes are small, typically twelve to eighteen students and no more than twenty-four, and rooms are carpeted to reduce noise. Seating is arranged like office meeting rooms to facilitate small group interaction. However, the learning environment is more than convenience; it begins there and progresses to educational substance, including the following:

Distributed Responsibility. The University of Phoenix classroom instructional model distributes the responsibility for teaching and learning to all participants. This "horizontal learning" model is supported by curriculum assignments that require interactive learning and emphasize the process of working toward solutions as much as the solutions themselves. Physical arrangements such as movable tables and/or breakout areas support these concepts.

Learning Groups and Study Groups. When a student enrolls in a University of Phoenix degree program, he or she immediately becomes a member of a learning group and a study group. Barring difficulties that might cause a student to drop back or drop out, the student will remain a member of his or her learning group throughout the degree program. The university-wide average size of learning groups is fourteen students. Each learning group is divided into study groups of three to four students. Although study groups can change membership as the learning group proceeds through the program, they usually retain their membership and develop strong ties among members, to the extent that many study groups become primary groups for life.

In fact, one of the most vital lifelong skills that a student acquires at the University of Phoenix is the ability to work in teams; the learning groups and study groups teach these skills every week throughout a degree program. Most colleges and universities emphasize individual achievement, not teamwork, despite the fact that working effectively in groups is vital in almost every organization. In traditional academia, the official word for the valuable skill of sharing information and ideas to arrive at a common solution to a problem is "cheating." Invariably, employers complain that the ability to work with others is missing from university graduates, and corporations then spend billions trying to develop in their employees skills that universities did their best to eradicate.

Learning Teamwork Skills. The University of Phoenix uses a variety of strategies to teach teamwork skills and attitudes. Just as in most workplace teams, students must find ways to divide the work equitably, ensure that each member fulfills his or her obligations, and fuse their individual efforts into a single final project. Study groups and study group assignments are not without their problems. Perhaps the most common complaint is that the "slacker" in a group gets more credit than he or she is due. Of course, these are the reasons why the University stresses the study group—it is precisely these problems that students will encounter at work. Indeed, the problems involved in achieving effective teamwork are what American businesses must solve if our economy is to compete with economies whose workers are skilled team workers.

Students on the Importance of Study Groups. "By working with other team members, you learn how to work with other people to accomplish a common goal. And I don't think you get that in a lot of other structured environments," says Eugene Maule, a University of Phoenix MBA student who is the president and CEO for Polymicro Technologies, a manufacturing firm of fiber-optic materials. "For those of us who have been in the workplace for a number of years, you realize in a hurry it really is a team effort, no matter what you're doing.... In a normal educational system, you don't get that. You take tests. You get points. You get percentages. You're really competing with one another...and that's a lot of nonsense. That's not how the real world works."

"You have people who are there because they really want to learn, so they'll take the initiative to meet outside of class, to work on projects together," Gary Sharum, Estimating Manager at Motorola in Phoenix, agrees. "I'm always working with teams of people, and committees, and situations like that. It really prepared me for the kind of environment I'm in now.... The study groups, the workshop style, is very typical of the environment that I work in now, so it really helped me prepare for a lot of things in management that I really hadn't had that much exposure to."

According to Gerald Koch, manufacturing engineering manager at Tandem Computers, Inc. in Cupertino, California, at the beginning of the program, the students in his group picked their own areas of expertise when dividing up the work. "But then we said, 'that's not going to work very well, because all you'll do is get better at what you're good at.' So we were forcing people to pick areas that they weren't good at, and that would be their segment of the project. The person who was already good at that area would act as a coach and mentor; it really only takes a little time, and you've developed a lot of people into well-rounded individuals."

Communication Skills: Oral and Written. The University of Phoenix's educational structure also forces students to develop the speaking and writing skills needed to function in the business world. At the University of Phoenix, it is not possible to graduate without being able to communicate effectively, both orally and on paper. Each week, different study groups investigate different aspects of the subject matter under study and must report on their findings to the rest of the class. Very quickly, students are forced to become comfortable making presentations. Bob Mitchell, a manager at Rocketdyne—who was working in instrument calibration before he enrolled at the University of Phoenix and who has been promoted three times since receiving his BSBA—was frightened of the oral presentations at first, but he quickly got over his shyness. "It forces a person to begin to use his or her verbal skills, to begin to interact. And within the thirteen months, I think we all became good speakers."

Equally valuable are the writing skills that students develop. There are no multiple-choice tests to fall back on—both bachelor's and master's students are required to turn out weekly papers for all of their classes, as well as comprehensive reports/theses on their research projects. To quote Linda Yokum, "If you're going to get your degree from the University of Arizona, you're going to read yourself through school. If you're going to get your degree from the University of Phoenix, you're going to write yourself through school."

"There's a lot of pressure to do a lot of writing," says Paul Hetrick, a section head with the electronics department at Hughes Aircraft. "There were also a lot of oral reports. And I think those two together really stimulated me into being able to write effectively and fairly rapidly, and being able to get up and really talk to a group—not a lot of memorizing and theory, but really doing it. Everything I wrote about and spoke about in class had a lot to do with my work at Hughes. The two played together. What you were doing for class you were really doing for work."

Bridging Theory and Practice: Education versus Training. When Bill Greer took his first computer class in his master's program at the University of Phoenix, he was thrilled to discover that his grade would depend upon his success at a real-world project. The class was assigned the task of developing a data-entry system for a nonprofit organization in Los Angeles that ran a residency system for elderly people. There was no computerized system to keep track of security deposits on the hundreds of apartments they rented all over the city—they were keeping their records on three-by-five cards. "Our job was to set up a computer system that not only worked, but that they also liked and would use. And our grade was dependent on the user's report on how it worked. It was great," says Greer. "Talk about reality-based!"

This story epitomizes a central tenet of the University of Phoenix's educational philosophy—that people learn better, and remember more of what they learn, if they apply it soon and repeatedly. This is especially true of adults, who tend to view education as a tool for solving problems or answering questions, rather than as an end in itself. If they cannot relate the contents of a course to their life experience, most adults will lose interest in it.

Applied Research Project. The University of Phoenix's hands-on, real-world orientation is perhaps best illustrated by the applied research project, the culmination of most University of Phoenix degree programs, in which the student investigates in depth a work-related topic of his or her choice. Students are encouraged to choose, and 75 percent do, a topic which relates to their professional lives, and which will be of use to the organizations for which they work. The University's *Alumni Impact Studies* consistently show that a majority of former students are of the opinion that their projects were important learning experiences and a source of personal pride. Many indicate that their projects addressed a significant problem in the organization that employs them, that it was effective in resolving the problem and that the organization benefited from its outcomes. Some students report that their projects also produced spectacular savings and/or increases in profits for the employing firm, nonprofit organization, or public agency.

Structure and Governance: Accountability and Effectiveness Rewarded

The University of Phoenix is unique in that it is both managed and governed. The University is a for-profit service corporation in which the Board of Directors sets policies and business strategies, and management carries out the policies and strategies. The faculty and its nominated academic governing body, together with the students and staff, oversee the quality of the educational services being delivered, and the teaching faculty and students create the dynamics of the teaching/learning process.

The characteristic which has had the greatest impact on the University's management and governance is its for-profit status. It was the first and remains the largest of the three or four regionally accredited for-profit universities in the country. The for-profit structure was chosen specifically to avoid many of the weaknesses the founders of the University had encountered during a lifetime working in educational institutions which were either non-profit or public. One of the most profound weaknesses they witnessed was the lack of financial discipline.

A for-profit structure cleared the way for innovations that were useful and accountable to the customer. For example, the educational process was conceived as a production function with the goal of producing a given level of educational services at the least cost. To accomplish this, it was necessary to define the learning outcomes the students needed to achieve and then to choose the most efficient mix of instructional processes to produce those outcomes.

A for-profit corporation that operates a university as a business is a hybrid entity; it must be operated at a profit to survive, and it also must maintain its accreditation by operating according to the canons of academic practice or it will not achieve its mission and, again, will not survive. The solution to this problem was to create parallel structures—a Board of Directors, composed of both businessmen and academics, and an academic governing body comprising faculty and administrators from the University's teaching ranks. The President is primarily responsible for business management, and the Academic Vice President is primarily responsible for academic management. In order to ensure that the Board had both managerial and academic oversight, the President is a member of the Board, and a public member of the Board chairs the academic body.

Today, the University is almost as small as it was at its beginning. It has built educational communities that are small, personal and physically and socially close to the students and to the communities in which they reside. Classroom environments are intimate and produce close professional and personal relationships between students and faculty. By staying small, the University has grown to be the largest private business school in the nation, without any of the more than 1,000 staff members, the 3,500 faculty members or the more than 30,000 students being aware of how large it has grown.

Quality Management at the University of Phoenix: Philosophy and System

As has already been stated, the University has made an organized pursuit of quality since its founding seventeen years ago. It took three years to get the first quality measurement—the End-of-Course Survey—installed and another three years to get it institutionalized and the results put to regular use. The task would never have been accomplished had not the university been managed as well as governed. Once the End-of-Course Survey was institutionalized, the other elements of the Academic Quality Management System fitted easily into the quality mosaic that is now part of the University culture and a source of pride to students, faculty and staff. Through the intentional development of organizational systems that maintain a vital tension between academic quality and integrity on the one hand, and accountability and good management practices on the other, the university encourages close inspection and measurement of all aspects of its educational services and outcomes.

The University of Phoenix measures everything that is or might possibly be important to the academic standards, practices and outcomes of the institution. A comprehensive evaluation research model continuously measures every detail of the University's inputs, processes and outcomes. One family of measures determines how well the practices of the University live up to established educational standards; another helps determine the utility of the university's academic standards in meeting the needs of society, particularly the needs of the labor force. Here, again, is meta-curriculum with a high degree of relevance. Students learn by example the mechanisms of assessment and accountability that they need to apply to their own work environments.

Registration Survey. This survey, completed during the registration process, asks students what factors influenced them to choose the University of Phoenix over alternative institutions, what major academic and professional goals they hope to achieve as they enroll in the University of Phoenix, what instructional methods are most effective in helping them to assimilate and retain knowledge, how they rate the overall effectiveness of the registration process and what their employers' opinions are of University of Phoenix programs.

Evaluation of Student Learning. The university places the primary responsibility for evaluating students' learning with the instructor and supports each instructor with the information, training and consultation necessary to function effectively in his/her role in the quality management's feedback system. The curriculum for each course sets out specific learning objectives and student evaluation is based on the achievement of these objectives, that is, a criterion-referenced evaluation. Criterion-referenced evaluation means that all students who achieve the learning objective will pass the course. Likewise, if no student meets the course objectives, none will receive a passing grade. In principle, there need be no grades of "F" or "D" awarded. For that matter, no grades need be awarded at all. However, there are both psychological and practical reasons making it beneficial for them to receive grades. Grades are a traditional form of feedback and provide a needed affirmation of performance. Moreover, many employers require grades as "proof" of achievement for their tuition subvention plan.

Peer and Administrative Reviews of Faculty Teaching. University of Phoenix faculty are assigned to classroom duties only after a rigorous selection and training process. In addition, in order to assure continued instructional excellence, there are two kinds of observational evaluations of faculty teaching. One is a peer review for the purpose of determining needs for additional training or mentoring; the peer review is strictly supportive, and no administrative action, other than arranging for training or mentoring, can come from the peer review process. The second kind is an administrative review, in which a member of the administrative staff visits the classroom for the purpose of determining if administrative action, including required training or dismissal, should be taken with respect to the faculty member.

Student End-of-Course Surveys: Objective Questions. Most colleges and universities employ some sort of end-of-course survey in which students rate their perceptions of educational delivery, educational content and administrative and environmental support. However, only a few institutions have exploited the full value of this information. Such surveys need to ask critical probing questions concerning curriculum, faculty and institutional support services. They should encourage participation from all students. The surveys should be administered apart from the normal classroom environment. The results should be aggregated across faculty, courses, programs, schools, years, and so on, and should be provided in a timely fashion to *all* educational stakeholders. Most important, all service providers should provide regular evidence that the information has been interpreted and put to use to improve the way things are done. Doing so will bring to bear appropriate forces to ensure that the interests of all stakeholders are represented in the process. None of the above should be confused with typical student end-of-course surveys as they are currently managed on most campuses. The empirically validated scales on the University of Phoenix survey, for example, contain over thirty scaled questions. Over 150,000 student-end-of course surveys are completed yearly. This constitutes an 85 to 90 percent response rate. Information from the student end-of-course survey is analyzed daily and is reported to faculty, area chairs and academic administrators in various regular and special reports.

Student Comment Analysis. If properly collected and analyzed, open-ended comments from students and faculty (typically written on the back of an end-of-course survey) possess several advantages over the more typical data from scaled questions. They carry more salience, significance and fidelity to the respondent's intentions. The downside to comment analysis is that some levels of analysis require the aggregation of a large number of comments over time and situations (computers are a must for any school with more than 5,000 students); and it takes some technical know-how to establish a knowledge-base or expert system to process them. The University of Phoenix developed a computerized knowledge-base comment analysis system that processes and analyzes over 200,000 student comments each year. (Comments are also typed and distributed immediately for rapid response to issues requiring immediate attention.) This system produces a family of periodic reports. Included in this report system is a detailed end-of-course comment profile for each faculty member, a report analyzing elements of curriculum on a course-by-course basis, a highly aggregated administrative report on university services and a cumulative comment profile for faculty, area chairs and program specialists. In its first two years of operation, the comment analysis system established itself as *the* earliest and most reliable source of information for operations and strategic planning.

The university's experiences with this kind of information has been very rewarding. Weak courses are identified in a matter of months rather than years. Using the comment analysis profiles, instructors are able to distinguish strengths and weaknesses in their teaching, and to distinguish trends of concern to many students from the background "noise" associated with all classroom teaching. Administrators are able to distinguish between isolated complaints and genuine problems and are, thereby, able to allocate resources more effectively.

Faculty End-of-Course Surveys. The university's requirement that faculty be qualified practitioners of the subjects they teach provides a valuable resource for assessing whether curriculum is up-to-date and technically sound. Faculty are also the University's best resource for determining whether students are professionally and academically prepared to benefit from their current educational experiences, and whether the learning environment and support services were as they needed to be. Similar to the student end-of-course survey, the scaled questions address curriculum and overall student preparation and the comments section adds salience, significance and fidelity to the respondent's intentions.

The Student Representative System. To enable the university to have direct and personal feedback from the students, most learning groups elect a student representative who represents the group's interests with the faculty member, university administration and staff. Student representatives at each campus meet as a group with the university's administration.

Comments to the Chairman. To provide a direct path to decision makers in the event that they have found other methods ineffective, each student and instructor in each course is provided with a postage-prepaid form which can be used to send confidential comments to the chairman of the board of the university; a similar form is sent each month with salary checks to all faculty and staff members. In addition, there is a comments hotline with an 800 number to a voice mail box. Students, faculty and staff send a regular stream of comments on problems, possibilities, suggestions for improvement, and praises for effective faculty and staff. Needed action is taken, and the person sending the comment is thanked and notified of the action.

Graduation Survey. Along with their diplomas, randomly selected students each receive a graduation survey. Graduates are asked to judge the quality of their University of Phoenix education by rating the university's educational and support services, indicating the degree to which the graduates met educational and professional goals, the degree of effectiveness of the instructional methods in helping them to learn and retain knowledge, how the University of Phoenix education compares in quality to the traditional colleges and universities they attended, what effect their research project had at their place of work and their opinions of the university's programs.

Adult Learning Outcomes Assessment (ALOA)

In an ideal world, meticulous attention to the delivery and evaluation of educational processes might vitiate the need for the measurement of outcomes. In the real world, schools need to know something about outcomes as well. Process evaluations provide an educational institution the ongoing information it needs to adjust its programs and services to provide the best outcomes possible. Outcomes assessments can serve to evaluate the efficacy of the processes themselves. In the case of the University of Phoenix, outcomes assessment is a family of interdependent measures designed to evaluate the extent to which the institution is accomplishing its fundamental mission and purposes, first in terms of achieving the desired learning outcomes for students, and second in terms of having a measurable and positive impact on the personal and professional lives of students. Each measure is designed to complement the whole to provide a multi-trait, multi-method view of the university's institutional effectiveness.

Comprehensive Cognitive Assessment of Achievement. This process begins with a three-hour entrance assessment that provides each student with a baseline appraisal of his or her current level of achievement in the major disciplines attendant to the degree being sought. A personalized five-to-ten page report mailed directly to the student provides a profile of his or her academic strengths and weaknesses, along with suggestions for putting the self-knowledge to good use. A similar assessment is administered when the student nears graduation. The post-assessment report permits students to see in specific terms where they place in relation to their peers, how much they achieved in relation to their prematriculation capabilities and where they now stand in each of the core disciplines attendant to their degree. A selection of students is also assessed periodically using appropriate nationally normed tests to establish baselines for comparing UOP students with students attending other institutions.[1] The interpretations and recommendations in the post-assessment report focus on lifelong learning, including self-guided learning, learning in the workplace and the value of cooperative learning.

Affective (Professional Values) Assessment. Every student also receives a pre- and post-assessment of affective growth. The assessment of affective growth is concerned primarily with the value one places on newly acquired professional knowledge and skills. Studies of successful professionals in a variety of disciplines show that they place a high value on certain attitudes and skills. Among these are: commitment to teamwork and cooperation; effective oral and written communications; self-confidence and a sense of competence; and critical thinking and evaluation skills. Learning objectives in these affective areas are integral to the university's curriculum. This comprehensive value assessment takes one hour to complete and contains empirically validated scaled, ranked and open-ended questions.

Alumni Impact. Alumni are surveyed to obtain a long-term view of the impact of their University of Phoenix education after having had sufficient time to integrate their learning with the demands of their current careers and personal responsibilities. Using empirically validated scales driven by the University's mission, the survey inquires of University of Phoenix alumni as to what factors influenced them to attend University of Phoenix, what major personal and professional goals they have achieved as a result of their University of Phoenix educational experience, how effective the University of Phoenix teaching/learning model was in helping them achieve their educational goals, the impact of their research project in their organization or profession and their employers' opinions of University of Phoenix programs since their graduation.

Faculty Impact. The professional lives of University of Phoenix faculty are significantly affected via their teaching experiences. Therefore, much like students and alumni, faculty are surveyed to identify their teaching goals and to determine the impact of teaching on their professional growth and development.

Employer Impact. A university serving working adults would be remiss were it not to assess the impact of its educational programs on the student's workplace. Under the employer impact portion of the ALOA, employers are surveyed to obtain an impartial, long-term view of the impact of the University's educational services on their employees, both as citizens and as professionals working to serve their organization's mission. This instrument contains scaled, ranked and open-ended survey questions. In-person interviews provide qualitative supplement to the information obtained from the surveys.

Research Project Assessment. Some degree programs require students to complete an applied research project in their core field. The integrative nature of these projects makes them an ideal source of information about students' ability to critically appraise and solve applied problems of direct relevance to their professional objectives. In the project assessment portion of ALOA, a review panel evaluates students' projects for their mastery of individual subject areas as well as for evidence that they integrate the many skills required to carry out an applied research study. Project reports are randomly selected for review using criterion-referenced rating and inter-rater reliability systems.

Use of the Above Information in a Process of Continuous Improvement. The large family of continuous evaluation research systems produces literally tens of thousands of electronic and paper reports to all stakeholders in the educational enterprise. This information is used in a process of continuous improvement applied to all university systems. As one of the principal sources of the information used to improve the efficiency, effectiveness and vitality of the university, students benefit from a meta-curriculum pertaining to customer service and product quality management.

We cannot say with certainty that other institutions would benefit by adopting all or part of the University of Phoenix educational model. We are certain that the UOP model evolved to its present form by paying strict attention to the needs of all constituents of the institution, by ensuring that change is continuous, and by rewarding efficient and constructive solutions to the naturally competing needs among constituents. We view these three points as the creative center of the university's educational model; it might be said that they are sufficient explanations of the path of the university's evolution.

Note

1. This is accomplished by administering the University of Phoenix assessment to a relatively small group of students at other universities and then statistically extrapolating the results.

Appendix B

"Diploma Mills": Higher Education's Red Herring

The True Nature of Diploma Mill Fraud

No doubt, diploma mills were once a danger before the problem was removed by professional licensing and the computer-based information systems that support the integrity of professional licenses throughout all fifty states. In order to protect consumers who use the services of licensed professionals, states have required practitioners to complete a required course of study, usually followed by an examination, prior to licensure, with continuing education needed for license renewal. One would assume this to be sufficient to protect consumers. To those dedicated to regulation however, one public danger remains: the fraudulent practitioner with a degree from a diploma mill. The claim is that fraudulent practitioners endanger the public and cast a negative light on the legitimate institutions that provide professional education programs. According to the higher education community and the staffs of the state higher education agencies, the best way to protect the public from diploma mills and their reprehensible products (the graduates) is to alert the public to the danger and to subject higher education to tighter state regulation.

The regulators' harangue against diploma mills provides good evidence that regulators assume that consumers of higher education are ignorant, gullible, and easily corrupted by the possibility of obtaining a degree simply by buying it. An excellent example of how this red herring is used is the excessive claim by the State Higher Education Executive Officers Association (SHEEO) that the diploma mill problem is undermining the public's perception of the value of higher education. A cursory review of the criticism of higher education during the last decade reveals that the diploma mill problem is not even on the list of reasons why the public is dissatisfied with higher education. What is on the list are complaints about the quality of the graduates of accredited colleges and universities, the increase in the cost of college tuition two to three times the rate of inflation, the needed for business and industry to re-educate ill-prepared college graduates, campus crime and the suppression of free speech on "politically correct" campuses.

In 1988, at the urging of SHEEO, the American Council on Education (ACE), higher education's major lobbying organization, published *Diploma Mills—Degrees of Fraud*, by David Stewart and Henry Spille. Stewart and Spille's thin research, undocumented assertions, and mushy logic provide conclusive evidence that "diploma mills" are higher education's ultimate diversionary tactic. Stewart and Spille claimed that, since salaries are tied to degree levels, "the nation is experiencing an explosive growth in diploma mills" (p. 13) and only rigorous state regulation of higher education can stop their proliferation. The authors' statistics on the supposed number of diploma mills fluctuate wildly. In 1950 there were more than 1,000; in 1959 there were 200 with a million customers; in 1960, the number had dropped to 25; in 1972 it was back up to 110; in 1984 it was 100; and in 1988 it had climbed back up to 357. In publishing these figures, the authors admit that "[S]ome of these sources [for the diploma mill figures] cannot be considered completely reliable in any empirical or scholarly sense." (p. 39) That is a gross understatement. The reality is that, except for the diploma mills licensed by the state of California,[1] the cited figures are inflated guesses.

There are a few "colleges" and "universities" that confer degrees after little or no instruction, but these institutions remain small in both number and in student population. They are easily recognized, because they are not accredited and they are vulnerable to rapid suppression by state consumer protection agencies. California, long called the "diploma mill state," has by far the largest number of substandard colleges and universities, because it licenses and thus legitimizes them. Without their state license, the sellers of bogus California degrees would have very few customers.[2]

The fact that Stewart and Spille's book is a travesty of scholarship has not deterred SHEEO or the ACE from their pursuit of "diploma mill" fraud. In October 1991, ACE announced that it had teamed up with the Council for Adult and Experiential Learning (CAEL) to conduct a study of quality assurance in adult learning. The major focus of the study was to identify the size and scope of abuses in substandard adult programs among which is the "explosion of 'diploma mills' in loosely regulated states." The authority for this assertion is none other than Dr. Spille, by now the national authority on diploma mills, who reported that the impetus for the study "has come from all sides" and that "there is a widespread, growing movement toward doing something about these problems." Contrary to this contention, most of the substandard adult programs are to be found on the campuses of traditional institutions and lack of quality assurance in traditional institutions is one of the major problems facing higher education. Almost all adult education occurs in traditional classrooms on traditional campuses and it is there one finds most of the substandard adult programs. They are substandard because they were not designed for the adult learner and are characterized by inappropriate curricula and ineffective instruction. Furthermore, most of the substandard adult outreach programs are offered by financially weak traditional institutions that use the income from the adult outreach programs to fund their on-campus operations.

Certainly, all adult programs can profit from an examination as to their "quality" but a study that begins with the conviction that the programs being studied are substandard is neither objective nor scholarly. Unless this conviction is put aside, the ACE-CAEL study cannot be taken seriously.

Notes

1. In California, institutions that do not meet the standards of regional accreditation are licensed by the state. Many California institutions offer degrees by mail in exchange for little more than the payment of fees.
2. These questionable California institutions have considerably enlarged their markets through extensive advertising in foreign publications. In countries with limited access to higher education, a degree from anywhere can be greatly desired. For example, in India, where university entrance is easy but passing the exams which qualify a student for a degree is difficult, unsuccessful candidates are proud to have their business cards note their university attendance with their name followed by "Failed B.A."

Appendix C

Summary of the Higher Education Licensing Regulations of the Fifty States

This table presents information in five columns: (1) the state; (2) methods of review of license applications; (3) the various restrictions which states place on licensure; (4) comments which help explain how the regulations are applied; and (5) codes for the eight restrictions widely practiced by state licensing agencies. It is evident from this summary that there will never be a national market in higher education until standard state regulations are mandated by the federal government or a system of national licensing is established. States without informatin are those that refused to respond to multiple inquiries.

Definitions of State Regulation Classification Codes

1. *Need requirement.*
   State requires that, to some extent, the applicant demonstrate that there is a need for the program. This is directly anticompetitive; it also gives the licensing authorities discretionary power.
2. *Competitors review application.*
   State permits potential competitors, usually state funded schools, to comment on the need for and merit of an application. This is inherently anticompetitive.
3. *Restrictive faculty requirement.*
   State requires full-time faculty, or other faculty restriction.
4. *Restrictive library requirement.*
   State has specific requirements concerning library services.
5. *Academic restrictions.*
   State has other nonlibrary requirements that can restrict access.

6. *Wide latitude given to decision-making body.*
   State has either general, nonspecific rules or processes which give great latitude, especially in denying applications, to the reviewing body.
7. *Accreditation restrictions.*
   State requires accreditation in a specific region, which can limit access.
8. *State will not license for-profit educational institutions.*

Summary of State's Higher Education Licensure Requirements

State	Methods of Review	Restrictions	Comments	Codes
Alabama	When the State of Alabama Dept. of Education receives an application for licensure, it will, if it appears the applying institution will probably qualify, forward that information to the Alabama Commission on Higher Education for its review and up or down vote.	* At least 50% of the courses must be taught by faculty employed full-time by the applying institution. * The Commission's review includes, but is not restricted to, the quality of academia support resources (library, laboratories, etc.).	Alabama's regulations for licensure are vague. The regulations are only four pages and allow the Commission to make arbitrary decisions regarding the grant of licensure.	3 6
Alaska	Applicants for licensure complete application and submit it to the Alaska Commission on Postsecondary Education. The Commission then reviews the application and arrangements are made for an on-site review. The application is placed on the agenda for the Commission's next meeting. Notification is made within 30 days.	* A student may not be required to be employed as a course requirement, unless the commission determines that it is reasonably necessary to gain practical experience. * Evidence must be presented that there is a need, based upon student interest; state, regional, national or international need.	Alaska's regulation's are restrictive but are open-minded about new educational methods. The following excerpt is included in their regulations: "A Postsecondary institution may develop innovative or flexible courses or programs that may depart from the requirements of this section, so long as those courses or programs provide instruction that fulfills both the stated institutional mission and the learning objectives of the enrolling student."	1 5 6
Arizona				

State	Methods of Review	Restrictions	Comments	Codes
Arkansas	Applicants for licensure submit application documents at least 60 days prior to the quarterly State Board of Higher Education meeting at which the application will be considered. The Board consists of ten members appointed by the governor. No more than three members of the Board may be graduates of any one state university or college, and no members of the Board of Trustees of any state university or college are eligible.	* The State Board of Higher Education shall make the final decision on all licensure requests. * Sufficient library resources figure in the licensure equation.	Arkansas' regulations are relatively open. While the Board has the final say on granting licensure, the composition of the board would seem to keep interschool rivalries out of the decision-making process.	4 6
California	The applying institution submits a Plan of Operation to the Council for Private Post-secondary and Vocation Education. After the application has been reviewed, an on-site review of an existing campus occurs. The on-site review team consists of members of existing accredited institutions already located in the state. After the on-site review, a decision is made to approve/disapprove the application.	* Members of the reviewing body are representatives of existing schools. * The presence of a library figures in the approval process. * The state requires a certain full-time faculty/student ratio. * The reviewing body is given a great degree of leeway in deciding whether a school should be approved/ disapproved.		2, 3, 4, 6
Colorado	The applying institution submits an application to the Colorado Commission on Higher Education. The Commission reviews the application and confirms the applying institution's accreditation. An on-site visit is then made and the school is approved/disapproved.	* Accreditation (or in the process thereof) by a nationally recognized accrediting agency is required.		7

State	Methods of Review	Restrictions	Comments	Codes
Connecticut	The Applicant for licensure submits an application to the Connecticut Commissioner of Higher Education. Comment is solicited from the academic community. The staff of the Department of Higher Education analyzes the resources available to support the proposed programs. The Commissioner then reviews the application and determines method for quality assessment. After a committee has completed its evaluation, a summary of findings and recommendations is prepared for consideration by the Board of Governors.	* The "Advisory Committee on Accreditation" is composed of representatives of accredited public and private institutions. * Proposals for new independent institutions are reviewed by the Commissioner in regard to need. * There shall be a reasonable ratio of full-time and part-time and adjunct faculty for each program. * Applying institutions shall be required to demonstrate that their libraries include sufficient printed material to support the needs of each proposed program.	Connecticut's regulations are very restrictive. Applying institutions must meet costly input standards. Connecticut leaves itself every opportunity to reject an application on all levels of the process. No out-of-state institutions are licensed in Connecticut.	1 2 3 4
Delaware				
District of Columbia	The Education Licensure Commission consists of five citizen members, each appointed by the Mayor for no more than two consecutive three-year terms. The Commission licenses, approves, and oversees all postsecondary educational institutions.	* The applying institution shall provide and maintain a collection of books, periodicals, newspapers, teaching aids, and other institutional materials.	Except for the issue of having a physical library, the District's regulations appear to be accommodating.	4

State	Methods of Review	Restrictions	Comments	Codes
Florida	The applying institution submits an application to the State Board of Independent Colleges and Universities. The Board reviews the application and an on-site visit is made. The Board then makes an up/down vote.	* Full-time faculty are required. * An applying institution must have a physical library. * The State Board is permitted a wide-range of latitude to approve/disapprove an application. * An applying institution must be accredited by a national agency.		3, 4, 6, 7
Georgia	The applying institution submits an application to the State Board of Education. The coordinator of Private College Standards reviews the application and, if the applying institution fits the criteria, an evaluation committee is appointed and further examines the application. If the committee deems it necessary, an on-site visit takes place. After the visit the committee then makes its recommendation for approval/rejection.	* The applying institution must show that there is need for such a program in the state. * The presence of a physical library plays a part in the approval process.	Georgia's regulations are very straight-forward. The two-part approval seems to be a way of weeding out "diploma mills." If the applying institution is able to get through the initial application, the second part appears to be a judgment call by the approving committee. There is also a section in Georgia's regulations for nontraditional programs. Georgia may be open to new ideas/concepts.	1 4 6
Hawaii				
Idaho				

State	Methods of Review	Restrictions	Comments	Codes
Illinois	Before submitting an application for approval, the applying institution must inform the Board of Higher Education of its intent to seek approval and the Board will publish the Notice of Intent in the agenda for its next meeting. The Board staff will seek the recommendations of a relevant consortium (composed of local college representatives) on the approval. The Board votes on the consortium.	* The consortium plays a big role in the approval process. * The applying intuition must show that there is need for such a program in Illinois.	Gaining approval is very difficult. The consortium system gives local institutions the opportunity to reject any institution's applications they see as threatening. Local institutions are given the opportunity to show that their schools already provide a similar service. This system is perhaps the most anti-competitive in the nation.	1 2 6
Indiana				
Iowa	An institution that wants to have a presence on the state level must register with Secretary of State. Registration is made by means of an application supplied by the secretary and in the time and manner prescribed by the secretary.	* The secretary of state is the sole decision maker in the application process.	Iowa's application rules are not very clear. The application for registration is 6 pages. Judging from the information the state supplied, if the secretary likes you, you're in. If not, you're out.	6
Kansas	The president of the institution contacts the office of the Kansas Board of Regents and arranges for a preliminary conference. The president then writes a letter of formal application for approval to the executive officer officially requesting the Board's consideration of the application.	* At least 70% of the full time equivalent faculty positions must be staffed by full-time employees. * The presence of a library plays an important part in the approval process.	Kansas' application procedures are straight-forward and clear. The regulations are obviously laid out to protect the state's residents against "diploma mills." Their real safeguard seems to be the requirement of a sufficient library. However, they do mention that if outside libraries are to play a part in the education of the students, it should be noted on the application.	3 4

State	Methods of Review	Restrictions	Comments	Codes
Kentucky	Application for licensure is in the form and manner prescribed by the Council on Higher Education. Within 30 days of receipt of a complete application the Council conducts a site visit. After the site visit the Council on Higher Education formally considers the application.	* Applying institutions must establish the need for the proposed program. The Council must agree that such a need cannot be reasonably met by colleges already located in Kentucky. * The presence of a library plays a part in the application process.	Kentucky's regulations are pretty clear-cut. The biggest hurdle to licensure is to establish the need for the programs to be offered by the institution seeking licensure.	1 2 4
Louisiana	The applying institution submits an application to the Louisiana Board of Regents. The Board reviews the information and determines the institution's status. The Board then makes an up/down vote.	There are no restrictions evident from the information provided by the state of Louisiana.		N/A
Maine	The applying institution notifies the Commissioner of the Department of Educational and Cultural Services six months prior to the start of a legislative session. The Commissioner then notifies the Presidents/Directors of all Maine institutions of higher learning about the application. After an application is submitted, the Commissioner forms a Review Committee consisting of individuals representing Maine's institutions of higher education. The Committee then submits a report to the Commissioner who makes his/her recommendation to the State Board of Education for approval/disapproval.	* State institutions are given the opportunity to comment on the applying institution's application. * A library and qualified librarians are part of the required elements of an applying institution. * Faculty are full-time employees.	The state's regulations are restrictive. Maine's Board of Education has given itself every opportunity to reject an application.	1 2 3 4 5

State	Methods of Review	Restrictions	Comments	Codes
Maryland	The applying institution submits an application to the Secretary of Higher Education. The Secretary and the Higher Education Commission review the application and the Secretary informs the applying institution of its approval/disapproval.	* Applying institution shall demonstrate the educational need to establish a campus in the state. The proposed program should not be duplicative of existing or planned programs. * At least one-third of the classes offered shall be taught by full-time faculty. * Adequate library shall be provided by the institution within state boundaries and within reasonable distance of the instructional site.	Maryland's process is restrictive and its standards are capital-intensive.	1 3 4
Massachusetts				
Michigan	The applying institution submits an application to the Michigan Board of Education. After a review by the Board and a written review by an ad hoc committee of scholars, the Board votes up/down.	* The applying institution must establish that there is a need in Michigan for such a program. * The ad hoc committee consists of representatives from existing Michigan institutions of higher learning. * The use of part-time faculty is discouraged.		1, 2, 3

State	Methods of Review	Restrictions	Comments	Codes
Minnesota	All institutions wanting to operate in Minnesota must submit an application to the Higher Education Coordinating Board. The Board reviews the application and gives an up or down vote on the applying institution.	* The school must provide an accessible library.	Minnesota's regulation seem to be accommodating and there are few restrictions. The following note is included in the application package: "Failure to meet any one of these criteria does not necessarily prevent a school from being approved. Rather a judgment shall be made on the basis of a pattern which in the whole supports a legitimate educational program, sufficient finances, and sound institutional policies and practices." It would appear they are willing to "bend the rules" for qualified institutions.	4
Mississippi	Institutions must submit an application to the Commission on College Accreditation. The Commission is composed of the Director of the Division of Junior Colleges in the State Dept. of Ed., along with a representative of the private colleges in the state. Applying institutions' applications are reviewed by the Commission and an up or down vote is taken.	* The Commission has adopted as its standards the criteria for accreditation of the Commission on Colleges, Southern Association of Colleges and Schools (SACS). Official accreditation by SACS is required for full accreditation with the Commission.	Approval without SACS accreditation is extremely unlikely. They do offer provisional accreditation--if the applying institution has a pending application with SACS.	1 7
Missouri	An application is submitted to the Coordinating Board of the State of Missouri. The Coordinating Board (which has representatives from public/private colleges) then reviews the application and approves/ disapproves it within 120 days.	* A certificate to operate a proprietary school is issued for a maximum of a one-year period and schools must be certified annually.	Missouri's regulations are very in-depth and cover a wide variety of scenarios involving different types of institutions. While approval is possible, the right of refusal rests with the Coordinating Board.	2 6

State	Methods of Review	Restrictions	Comments	Codes
Montana	See comments	See comments	Montana's regulations do not apply to an accredited institution. Any program or course of instruction of an institution accredited by a national or regional accrediting agency recognized by the board of regents of higher education are exempt from Montana's regulations. Notification of such recognition must be given to the board.	
Nebraska	Applying institutions must submit an application to the Nebraska Coordinating Commission for Postsecondary Education. The application must include legal documents illustrating the institution's accreditation in the states in which it currently operates. The staff reviews the application and a decision is made within 30 days.	* There are no restrictions evident from the information provided by the state of Nebraska.	Nebraska's licensure process seems to be straightforward and open.	
Nevada				
New Hampshire	See comments	* The faculty shall have full-time employees. * The institution shall rely on its own library for its basic collection. * The applying institution shall take into consideration the impact its presence will have on other educational institutions.	In lieu of conducting its own evaluation, the New Hampshire Commission of Higher Education shall accept accreditation by a regional accrediting association, by agencies listed by the U.S. Secretary of Education for its accreditation of college degree granting programs or curriculum offered by an institution of higher education or by professional or specialized accrediting agencies recognized by the U.S. Secretary of Education.	1 3 4 7

State	Methods of Review	Restrictions	Comments	Codes
New Jersey	The licensure and Approval Advisory Board consists of representatives from each of New Jersey's public institutions as well as from each of the private institutions located in the state. The Board reviews the applying institution's application and makes a recommendation to the Chancellor for approval/disapproval.	* Faculty members should be full-time employees. * The presence of a library figures in the approval process.	The application process in New Jersey is based solely on the decision of the Licensure Board which is made up of members representing competing institutions. While the regulations seem straightforward, it is clear that the Board has the final say on whether licensure will be granted. No out-of-state institutions are licensed in New Jersey.	1 2 4 6
New Mexico	Applications for licensure must submit an application to the State Commission on Higher Education. The Commission then reviews the application and surveys the institution, its curriculum, and its physical facilities. If the Commission feels requirements have been satisfactorily met, it will issue a certificate of approval	No restrictions are evident from this literature. However, out-of-state proprietary schools as defined in some section of the act (not found in the files) are not subject to the act's rules.		N/A
New York	The applying institution submits an application to the Deputy Commissioner for Higher & Continuing Education. The application is then passed on to the Regents of the State University of New York for review approval/disapproval.	* An applying institution must demonstrate that there is a need for its program in the state. * The presence of a library figures in the approval process.	New York's application process is restrictive. The applying institution must illustrate that there is a need for the program in the state. The decision on whether there is a "need" is decided by representatives of the institutions already located in New York, thus giving them the opportunity to eliminate any possible competition. No out-of-state institutions are licensed in New York.	1 4

State	Methods of Review	Restrictions	Comments	Codes
North Carolina	An officer from the applying institution must meet with the President of the University of North Carolina to discuss standards and procedures for application. The applying institution then submits an application and a team of examiners visits the school's current site. The examiners give their recommendations to the President and a recommendation is then passed on to the Board of Governors. They make the final decision.	* The institution should rely on its own library for its basic collection.	North Carolina's regulations are restrictive. The application process is made directly through the University of North Carolina system. According to the records provided by North Carolina, very few licenses have been granted to private institutions.	2 4
North Dakota	Applying institutions submit an application to the Commissioner of Higher Education. The application is reviewed by a board and a decision is passed down.	* The applying institution must demonstrate the value of the program to North Dakota.	North Dakota's application process is open. The minimum criteria for an applying institution is very basic. Politics do not seem to play a part in the process. North Dakota's regulations state that regulations are not in place to "hinder legitimate educational innovation."	1
Ohio	The applying institution submits an application to the Ohio State Board of School and College Registration. Staff reviews the application and makes a recommendation to the Chancellor. The Chancellor then passes on his/her recommendation to the Board. The applying institution appears at a public hearing and a decision is made by an up or down vote.	* The applying institution shall maintain a sufficient library. Not less than 15,000 volumes. * Full-time faculty members are required.	Ohio's application process seems to be a bureaucratic labyrinth. The process appears to give the state of Ohio endless opportunities to reject an application.	3 4 5 6

State	Methods of Review	Restrictions	Comments	Codes
Oklahoma	The applying institution submits an application to the Oklahoma State Regents for Higher Education. After a site visit, an up or down vote is taken by the Regents.	* An applying institution must demonstrate that there is a need for such a program in Oklahoma which is not already being met by an existing Oklahoma institution. * An institution must be non-profit in order to be eligible for accreditation.	Oklahoma's application process is very restrictive. It does not permit for-profit institutions.	1 6 8
Oregon	The applying institution must obtain state authorization through the Office of Educational Policy and Planning, which will conduct an onsite inspection of the applicant institution and will interview students, employees, and officials of the institution. A hearing will then be held, open to the public, and with a representative of the institution present, to determine whether to approve/disapprove the applicant institution. Failure to appear or adequately answer questions is a basis for disapproval of the application.	* Information from other bodies also examining the institution, usually accrediting agencies, may accompany the application requested by the Office. This information "will be used as the Office considers appropriate, and the interpretations of other bodies create no presumption concerning any decision to be reached by the Office."		6
Pennsylvania	The applying institution submits an application to the Pennsylvania Department of Education. A team reviews the application and makes an on-site visit. It makes a recommendation to the Secretary of Education for a decision on the request.	* An applying institution must have a minimum protective endowment of at least $500,000. * The institution cannot operate for-profit	Pennsylvania's application is very restrictive. It does not permit for-profit institutions.	8

State	Methods of Review	Restrictions	Comments	Codes
Rhode Island	The applying institution submits a proposal to the Office of Higher Education. The proposal is reviewed by the presidents of all the other higher education institutions in the state, external consultants, and the Commissioner of Higher Ed. The Commissioner makes his/her recommendation to the Board of Governors. The Board makes the final decision.	* Full-time faculty must exist in an acceptable ratio to part-time faculty.	Rhode Island's process is somewhat restrictive. The fact that the presidents of existing institutions get to comment on an application does not bode well for an applying institution.	2 3
South Carolina	The applying institution has a preliminary conference with the Commission on Higher Education to discuss the standards for implementing licensure. A formal application is submitted and reviewed and a decision is made whether to give the institution temporary licensure. An on-site visit is made and the Commission on Higher Ed. makes a recommendation for approval/disapproval.	* The proportion of full-time staff and student/teacher ratio shall be acceptable. * Students must have access to an adequate library.	South Carolina's application process is straightforward and does not appear to be extremely restrictive; they do allow themselves a bit of leeway for making a decision on an institution's application. Also, an institution accredited by the Southern Association of Colleges and Schools is exempt from the state's review.	3 4 6
South Dakota	An applying institution submits an application to the South Dakota Department of Education. The S.D. Secretary has the final say on licensure.	* There are no restrictions evident from the information provided by the state of South Dakota.	South Dakota's licensure regulations are very brief. They do not mention restrictions, except for the denial of approval for people who are known to be of poor character. The decision is based on the opinion of one person.	

State	Methods of Review	Restrictions	Comments	Codes
Tennessee	For authorization, an institution must apply to the State Committee on Postsecondary Educational Institutions. The Committee may then initiate and conduct an onsite review and/or investigation. Subsequently, it will approve or disapprove the authorization.	* Institutions with the word “college” or “university” in their names must be accredited by SACS, the American Association of Bible Colleges (AABC), or meet all criteria of an appropriate accrediting agency as determined by an external review team. *Undergraduate degree programs must devote at least 25% of their programs to general education courses. * Graduate degree programs must provide an experienced research staff to direct graduates' research papers.	Tennessee's policies appear restrictive.	5 7
Texas	The applying institution submits an application to the Texas Higher Education Coordinating Board. After an on-site review and vote by the Commission, the request for licensure is either approved or denied.	* Texas recognizes only SACS accreditation. * There must be at least one full-time faculty member for each program. * The institution shall have its own library.	Texas’ regulation is very restrictive and they require SACS accreditation.	3 4 7
Utah	Within 30 days after applicants for licensure receive the registration form, the State Board of Regents will either issue a certificate, request more information, or conduct an onsite visit. NOTE: This is for the re-registration.	* In order to be registered in Utah, a proprietary school must have a “significant presence with in the state and conduct significant educational services affecting the people of the state.	Utah specifies a limitation of the Board's authority. Except for stipulations made regarding registration, “the Board [may not] regulate the content of individual courses or regulate the day-to-day operations of a proprietary educational institution.”	

State	Methods of Review	Restrictions	Comments	Codes
Vermont	An applying institution submits an application to the State Board of Education. After review by an independent reviewer, a final decision is made.	* There are no restrictions evident from the information provided by the state of Vermont.	Vermont's licensure process appears to be very accommodating. However, the state requires a "self-study" that is reviewed by an appointed panel, and there is no way to know what the standards will be.	
Virginia	An applying institution submits an application to the State Council of Higher Education for Virginia. After staff review and recommendation, the application is passed on to the Council for its review. Following a site visit, a decision to approve/ disapprove is made by the Council.	* At least 50% of the faculty should be full-time. * The institution shall have 1 full-time faulty for every 25 students. * The institution shall have an on-site library.	Virginia's licensure process is very restrictive. Aside from the mentioned restrictions, the process of gaining approval seems arduous.	4 5 7
Washington	Following a staff review of the application, an on-site visit and a review by outside experts, a recommendation is made to the executive director. The executive director makes the final decision.	* 20% of the curriculum must be taught by full-time faculty. * The presence of a library figures in the approval process.	Except for the mentioned restrictions, Washington's application process appears to be accommodating. Since the review process is done by staff, politics are not likely to play large role in the process.	3 4
West Virginia	An applying institution has a preliminary meeting with the Board of Regents. The Chancellor of the West Virginia Board of Regents appoints a visiting committee. The committee makes its recommendation to the Chancellor and he/she makes the final decision.	* There are no restriction evident from the information provided by the state of West Virginia.	West Virginia did not provide information about minimal requirements.	
Wisconsin				
Wyoming				

Appendix D

Differential Treatment of Proprietary Schools Under Title IV of the Higher Education Act

Prior to 1992, the Congress, unlike the Department of Education, tried assiduously to avoid different treatment of for-profit and not-for-profit institutions. However, in efforts to curb perceived abuses in the federal student aid program, the 1992 reauthorization of the Higher Education Act incorporated several provisions, under Part H of Title IV, which de facto place specific burdens on the for-profit institutions. Additionally, new language was added to the definition of "proprietary" school that imposes certain criteria that apply only to such schools.

The language is sufficiently broad to allow the secretary great discretion in the regulatory process. For example, in language dealing with ownership in Part II, it is unlikely that the Secretary would require a personal bond from the president of a not-for-profit institution, although the statute allows it and makes no differentiation between for-profit and not-for-profit institutions. The bottom line is that the impact of the legislative language on proprietary schools is in the hands of the secretary. A secretary favorable to such schools could govern them almost identically to not-for-profit schools. On the other hand, the secretary has the authority, in several areas, to prescribe more rigorous standards for proprietary schools.

The chart below indicates specific legislative differences between the requirements for not-for-profit and for-profit institutions.

Issues	Not-For-Profit Schools	For-Profit Schools
Definition	The definition of an "institution of higher education," as defined in section 481 of the Higher Education Act and specifically for the purposes of student financial aid programs, includes proprietary schools. The more general definition contained in section 1201 of the act mandates that a school must be a not-for-profit institution.	The unique requirements for for-profit schools in the definition include: 1) an eligible program of training to prepare students for gainful employment in a recognized occupation; 2) accredited by a nationally recognized agency or association approved by the secretary, pursuant to Part H; 3) no more than 85% of its revenues from student financial aid program administered by the Department of Education; and 4) at least two years of operation.
Financial Responsibilities	Part H of the Higher Education Act was written as a school integrity provision. While not-for-profit and for-profit schools are not specifically delineated, many of the references, such as school ownership and control, do not fit the model of a not-for-profit institution. A major change in proposed regulations was brought about because not-for-profit schools do not maintain a greater than one-to-one ratio of assets to liabilities. Hoping to eliminate several proprietary schools from eligibility to participate in the student aid programs, the Department of Education had originally proposed upping the ratio to 1.25 to 1, only to learn that not-for-profit schools could not meet that criteria. The 1:1 ratio was maintained.	Part H of Title IV mandates a number of provisions intended to limit proprietary schools' participation in student financial aid programs. While such schools are not singled out, the scenarios described apply to for-profit schools far more than they do to not-for-profit institutions. The secretary may require financial guarantees from an institution, or from individuals who exercise control over an institution, participating or seeking to participate in the programs, in a sufficient amount to protect the government against potential liability. Clearly the concept of individual owners rarely applies to not-for-profit institutions. The law also allows the secretary to require owners or controllers of institutions to assume personal liability for financial losses to the federal government, students, and other program participants. Such individuals could be subject to the monetary and criminal penalties under the act.

Index